THE
LITTLE
BOOK
OF
GLASGOW

GEOFF HOLDER

The
History
Press

First published 2011

The History Press
The Mill, Brimscombe Port
Stroud, Gloucestershire, GL5 2QG
www.thehistorypress.co.uk

British Library Cataloguing in Publication Data.
A catalogue record for this book is available from the British Library.

ISBN 978 0 7524 6004 8
Typesetting and origination by The History Press
Printed in Great Britain
Manufacturing managed by Jellyfish Print Solutions Ltd

INTRODUCTION

Glasgow. Complex. Contradictory. Chaotic. An architectural wonderland. A sporting Valhalla. A cultural and economic dynamo. A mess of historical and contemporary social poisons, from poverty to sectarianism. The former second city of the Empire. The 'dear green place'. The heart of Red Clydeside. The home of heavy industry. The anti-Edinburgh.

Glasgow is one of the great European cities; which means there is so much to say about it that this book could easily have been twice the length. Or, alternatively, an entirely different *Little Book of Glasgow* could have been written, stuffed to the gills with a completely variant set of trivia, facts, bizarre historical titbits, artistic achievements and peculiarities of animal and human behaviour. Here is my selection of oddities and quiddities plucked from space and time. If you do know Glasgow, I hope it will shine a light on areas that were previously in shadow, and if you are new to the city, welcome to its leftfield wonders.

My thanks go out to all the librarians without whom the writing of this book would have been a horror beyond comprehension, and also to the authors of the many splendid books that I have plundered for items juicy or bejewelled.

The images have been taken from a number of Victorian and Edwardian sources, including *Punch*, *The Scottish Nation Illustrated*, *Pearson's Magazine*, *The Quiver* and *The Biographical Dictionary of Eminent Scotsmen*.

1

PLACES – HERE & NOW, THEN & THERE

PREHISTORIC DAYS

In 1938 Ludovic MacLellan Mann uncovered what he thought was a prehistoric druid complex at Knappers Quarry off Great Western Road. His entirely bogus reconstruction of 'Scotland's Stonehenge' attracted thousands of visitors and earned him the derision of archaeologists. Recent reassessment has shown that although he may have been away with the fairies when it came to druids and ritual sacrifice, he may have actually found a Bronze Age timber monument. Sadly the site was obliterated by high-rise housing after the Second World War.

Urban development has eradicated most of Glasgow's prehistoric sites. As late as 1973 a standing stone on Boydstone Road was removed for road widening. The Kelvingrove Museum has a very good display of grave goods found in prehistoric burial cists.

Also in the museum are more than 250 items recovered from a crannog in Bishop's Loch in about 1905. Crannogs are dwellings erected in lakes, and this one was occupied in the Early Iron Age, from about 700 BC.

WHAT DID THE ROMANS EVER DO FOR US?

Between AD 142 and 144 the Romans built the turf-and-earth Antonine Wall between the Firth of Clyde and the Firth of Forth – the narrowest 'neck' of Scotland. The wall and the accompanying Military Way passed just north of Glasgow, with several stretches still extant, and a fort can be seen at Bearsden. The Hunterian

Museum has an excellent collection of inscribed stones from the wall. The Antonine Wall was abandoned after only twenty years, the army withdrawing south to Hadrian's Wall.

Part of the Antonine Wall runs through the course of Cawder Golf Club, formerly Cawder House, on the banks of the Kelvin. The clubhouse holds a legionary stone inscribed, 'The 2nd Legion Augustus built this'.

THE EARLIEST GLASGOW – ST KENTIGERN

Little is known of Glasgow in the Dark Ages. A church was founded here in the sixth century by St Kentigern, also known more familiarly as St Mungo. The site was where the cathedral stands now, at the time on the banks of the fast-flowing Molendinar, a mile north of the sluggish Clyde. From this tiny beginning grew a Christian settlement which slowly gained in political power and commercial acumen.

Legend has it St Mungo performed four miracles in Glasgow, commemorated on the City of Glasgow's coat of arms, depicting a tree with a bird perched on its branches and a salmon and a bell on either side.

What everyone 'knows' about St Kentigern derives from a hagiography (the biography of a saint) written by a Cumbrian monk called Jocelyn of Furness Abbey, almost six centuries after Kentigern died. Jocelyn himself admitted his *Life of Kentigern* was partly based on legend and invention. The real power behind the hagiography was Bishop Jocelin, who in the 1180s was determined to have Kentigern declared a saint – and a biography stuffed with miracles and divine wonders was part of his propaganda campaign. Once the Pope sanctified Kentigern, Glasgow became a magnet for spiritual pilgrims, enhancing the town's reputation – and bringing in piles of donations. As far as medieval cathedrals and bishops were concerned, medieval saintliness was about two things – power and money.

MEDIEVAL GLASGOW AND THE CATHEDRAL

Glasgow in the Middle Ages was little more than a village, however, it did have a cathedral, and that made it a centre of power.

The cathedral was almost not sited in Glasgow at all. The obvious first choice was Govan, which in the eleventh century had a pre-eminent religious status within the area. But when David I became king, he rejected Govan because it was associated with the previous royal dynasty. David needed his own power base, and so sometime between 1113 and 1124 he created the position of the Bishop of Glasgow, and started building a cathedral to be the centre of the diocese. Govan was sidelined and declined into insignificance.

Glasgow's elevation to a bishopric, thus becoming the principal church in the West of Scotland, marks the moment the town started to become a force in the land. Then, in 1175, it was made a Burgh of Barony, meaning it could control its own trade and politics. The older Royal Burghs of Dumbarton and Rutherglen had their noses put out of joint – but Glasgow had arrived, and power politics in Scotland would never be the same again.

The diocese of the Bishop of Glasgow stretched all the way to the Solway Firth and the English border, incorporating 200 parishes and generating huge sums in rents and other income. Within Glasgow itself the bishops had all the power and prestige of a great lord – basically, they ruled Glasgow and what the bishop said, went.

Several serious fires and the scale of the building project meant that the cathedral was a construction site for centuries. The first cathedral was consecrated in 1136. What we see today is largely the third building, mostly built in the thirteenth century, although major alterations continued for another 100 years.

GLASGOW CATHEDRAL – SOME FACTS

The cathedral is partly built on a steep slope, a site no sensible mason would have chosen. The reason was simple – it was erected over the traditional spot of Kentigern's grave, and piety trumped practicality.

The cathedral was known as 'the Pride of Lanarkshire', but the extended building programme also brought comparisons with Penelope's Web from Greek mythology – for neither would ever be finished.

Part of the south transept was called the Dripping Aisle after a persistent leak.

The cathedral was built as a pilgrimage shrine for the relics of St Kentigern. The cult of St Kentigern was expressly modelled on that of the English martyr St Thomas à Becket, and strong corporate links were forged between the cathedrals of Glasgow and Canterbury. Glasgow even ended up with some of Becket's relics.

Relics were a key part of the attraction of visiting a medieval cathedral, as their presence was supposed to create healing miracles. By the fifteenth century Glasgow Cathedral had purchased or otherwise acquired well over twenty significant relics, making it the premier pilgrimage destination in Scotland and northern England. Among its alleged treasures were:

A piece of the True Cross

Part of Jesus' manger from the stable at Bethlehem

Some hairs from the head of the Blessed Virgin Mary, plus a piece of her girdle

Bones from St Bartholomew (one of the original twelve Apostles), St Thomas of Canterbury, St Magdalene, St Ninian, St Eugene, St Blaze, and St Kentigern (and his mother, St Thenew)

Part of St Martin's cloak (the Bible describes him cutting up his cloak to clothe a beggar)

A small phial containing the breast milk of the Virgin Mary

Sadly all these items, along with reliquaries of silver and gold decorated with precious stones, all vanished after the Reformation – some were taken for safekeeping to Paris, where they disappeared following the French Revolution.

The senior team at the cathedral were called prebends or canons. Each prebend had a substantial stone-built manse or town house on one of the principal streets such as Rottenrow, Drygate or Castle Street. Provand's Lordship, now a museum, is the last remaining of these privileged dwellings.

By 1484 Glasgow was elevated to an archbishopric, the high-water mark in the city's ruthless climb through the layers of medieval religious power-politics. The move really miffed the Archbishop of St Andrews – the ancient diocese of St Andrews had been trying to take over or limit the power of the upstart Glasgow for 300 years.

In 1545 two rival archbishops, from St Andrews and Glasgow, met at the door of the cathedral, each claiming superiority over the other. All concerned were deeply learned men of the cloth, and so the dispute was solved in the obvious way – by a punch-up.

At one point the two archbishops were clubbing each other with their respective archiepiscopal crosses. All this infighting was rendered moot when the bishops were swept away by the Scottish Reformation in 1560.

From the 1580s the gloom-filled crypt, formerly the focus for Catholic saint-devotion, was used as a place of worship for members of the Barony parish, effectively splitting the cathedral into two Protestant churches. When the Barony parishioners moved out in 1798 they filled the crypt with a layer of earth and used it as a burial ground, complete with gravestones and iron railings. This state of affairs continued until 1835, when the crypt was cleared out and restored to its original condition.

During the Second World War the crew of a motor torpedo boat crew found a 'lucky' ladybird on board. When they were subsequently attacked and sunk, all the men managed to survive. In gratitude they presented a canopied chair to the cathedral – with a tiny decoration of a ladybird in one corner.

GLASGOW CASTLES

They may not be well known, but Glasgow's castles are out there and can be visited.

Bothwell Castle in Uddingston is a magnificent and massive medieval ruin cared for by Historic Scotland. Highly recommended.

Crookston Castle off Brockburn Road is Glasgow's best 'unknown' castle, with remains from the twelfth through to the fifteenth centuries. It was the first property presented to the National Trust for Scotland (in 1931) and is now cared for by Historic Scotland.

Mearns Castle near Newton Mearns is a fifteenth-century restored tower, now partly incorporated in the Maxwell Mearns parish church.

Quite a bit remains of the seventeenth century L-plan tower house of **Gilbertfield Castle**, which still totters south of Cambuslang.

THIRTEEN LOST CASTLES

It is hard these days to think of Glasgow as a city of castles, and indeed there was never anything here as grand as the royal fortresses of Edinburgh or Dumbarton, or even the castellated piles of the great nobles. But, once upon a time, Glasgow was awash with smaller castles and towers. Here are some of those that have vanished.

1. The principal castle was the Bishop's Castle, which stood where the Royal Infirmary does today. More of a fortified tower than a fortress, it was built before 1258 and fell into decline after the Reformation, its stones finally being carted away in 1752 (to build the first Saracen's Head Inn).

2 & 3. The medieval bishops of Glasgow also had a moated castle and hunting lodge at Lochwood, Easterhouse, and a residence on the west bank of the Kelvin, known as Partick Castle. The former was destroyed in 1579, while parts of the latter survived until the early nineteenth century.

4. Renfrew Castle was the ancestral home of what later became the royal House of Stuart, although every stone vanished centuries ago. The heir to the throne of the United Kingdom still has official claim on the jurisdiction, which is why one of Prince Charles' titles is 'Baron of Renfrew'.

5. Rutherglen Castle saw several sieges and changes of ownership until it was burned after the Battle of Langside in 1568. The last remains were removed in the eighteenth century.

6. There were three successive Pollok Castles: the first a wooden structure built in 1160, the second a stone tower erected in 1270 and the final a larger castle constructed in about 1500. Although replaced by the Georgian mansion of Pollok House in 1752, part of the last castle remained standing until a fire in 1882.

7. Drumsagard Castle, a fourteenth-century nobleman's residence near Cambuslang, was demolished in the 1770s and the stones reused to build a farm.

8. The Doomster or Moot Hill, which was probably a twelfth-century Norman motte for a timber castle, used to be a prominent feature north of Govan Cross. It was removed in the early nineteenth century to make way for a dyeworks.

9. Part of a seventeenth-century tower house survived until 1870 on Main Street in Gorbals. The site is now partly occupied by the Citizens Theatre.

10. The sixteenth-century Peel of Drumry in Drumchapel was destroyed by Glasgow Corporation in 1958.

11. After undergoing many changes over the centuries, Castlemilk Castle met the corporation's wrecking ball in the 1960s.

12. Fifteenth-century Farme Castle in Rutherglen was ruinous by the late nineteenth century. The keep was finally demolished in the 1960s – by Glasgow Corporation.

13. The last castle demolished by the council was the fifteenth-century Cathcart Castle in Linn Park, which was reduced to its foundations in 1980.

THE NAME 'GLASGOW'

The persistent popular belief is that the city's name is derived from a Gaelic phrase, *Glas-cu*, meaning 'dear green place'. But as the man said, 'it ain't necessarily so'.

For a start, no-one was speaking Gaelic in the Glasgow area. Gaelic was brought over to the west coast of Scotland by the Dalriadans of Ireland in the Dark Ages. People in early Glasgow, which was part of the enormous Kingdom of Strathclyde stretching to beyond the Mersey, would have spoken a version of Welsh.

Secondly, there is the difficulty of authentic spelling: the name was written as 'Glasgu' in 1116, 'Glasgow' in 1158 and 'Cleschu' in 1185. Depending on what etymologist you read, the name could therefore include the Old Welsh for 'river', or 'blue', or even 'greyhound'.

So in truth, no-one really knows what 'Glasgow' actually means.

PLACE-NAME PECULIARITIES

The name Trongate is derived from the 'tron', the beam used to measure the weight of all goods brought into the city for sale. Trongate first appears on a document in 1560.

'Gate' did not mean 'gate', as in a door in a wall. A Scottish 'gate' was a main thoroughfare, as in Bridgegate, 'the road to the bridge', and Gallowgate, 'the road to the gallows'.

If you look around the junction of Byres Road and Dowanside Road you will see the inscription 'Victoria Cross'. This is a relic of an attempt to rename Byres Road in honour of Queen Victoria – the attempt foundered on local resistance, and Victoria Cross was never instigated.

Nineteenth-century Bath Street was home to many doctors, and was therefore known as the Valley of the Shadow of Death.

SOME UNUSUAL STREET NAMES

Mossend has more names inspired by mythology than any other area in Glasgow, with streets named for Neptune, Midas, Phoenix, Hermes, Leander, Triton and Pegasus. Renfrew boasts Hercules and Lysander, while Springburn, rather appropriately as it was a manufactory of locomotives, has Vulcan and Atlas. Athena, Neptune and Minerva manifest in Tannochside, Govan and the city centre respectively.

Apollo Path and Gemini Grove in Holytown are named after American space missions (which were of course named after figures from mythology).

Exotica: Bellshill boasts a Babylon Road, there's a Kew Gardens in Viewpark, and Chryston is home to The Everglades.

Street names in Knightswood and Temple, drawing on the area's alleged links with the Knights Templar, are a rich skein of medieval references. You can find arms and armour: Mace,

Glaive, Gorget, Chaplet, Tabard and Baldric; job descriptions: Crusader, Minstrel, Templar, Thane, Palmer, Herald, Warden and Pikeman; and a slew of associated words such as Moat, Turret, Friarscourt, Monksbridge and Saxon. The streets also forge a thematic connection with Sir Walter Scott's medieval romance *Ivanhoe* – with character names such as Ivanhoe himself, plus Rowena, Baldwin, Cedric and Waldemar.

Street names with supernatural associations include Bogleshole Road in Cambuslang (a bogle is a spirit), Warlock Drive and Road in Bridge of Weir, Fairyknowe Court and Gardens in Bothwell, and Witchwood Court in Coatbridge. The path now occupied by Bellgrove Street in the East End used to be known as Witch Loan.

One-off streetname oddities include: Fifty Pitches Road in Hillington, Tak-ma-doon Road in Kilsyth, Jacob's Ladder in Overtown, Grudie Street and Sielga Place in Easterhouse, Hurly Hawkin in Bishopbriggs, Fossil Grove in Kirkintilloch,

Gowkthrapple near Wishaw, Wamba Avenue in Westerton, Ulundi Road in Johnstone and, in Temple, a certain Hemlock Street.

Twenty-four different species of birds appear in Glasgow street names:

Cormorant
Crow
Curlew
Eagle
Falcon
Finch
Heron
Kestrel
Lapwing
Lark
Mallard
Peacock
Plover
Raven
Robin
Sheldrake
Swallow
Swan
Swift
Teal
Tern
Thrush
Whimbrel
Wren

In contrast, the only animal on display is in Viewpark, which has a Gopher Avenue.

STREET STATISTICS

In the full index of current streets in Greater Glasgow, the most common name is 'Victoria', with 58 examples.

The second most popular street name is 'Park', with 44 entries, followed closely by the 42 uses of 'Station'. Of the latter, 32 are Station Roads.

'Main Street' appears 33 times, 'High Street' twelve times, 'Mill' scores 29, 'Maxwell' 28, 'Morar' 26 and 'Meadow(s)' 21. Other high achievers are 'Maple' (24 times), 'Manse' (20 examples) and 'Manor' with 13 entries. Of course, some of these high scores come from the modern tendency to use the same root-name many times, as in Maple Street, Way, Road, Avenue, Court and so on.

There are no street names or place-names in Glasgow beginning with the letter 'X'.

LISTED BUILDINGS

There are 1,824 listed buildings in Glasgow, although 'building' isn't always the right word, as the range of 'items of architectural merit' includes entire terraces, as well as lamp-posts, postboxes and former police boxes. In fact, 15 per cent of all listed buildings in Glasgow are Grade A, which means they are of national or international importance.

As you might expect the A-listed buildings include many well-known attractions and historic buildings such as the People's Palace, the Kelvingrove Art Gallery and Museum, Provand's Lordship, the Gallery of Modern Art, the Necropolis and the Bridge of Sighs, the Kibble Palace in the Botanic Gardens, Pollok House, the Tolbooth steeple, Crookston Castle, Provan Hall, and the National Trust for Scotland's Hutcheson's Hospital on Ingram Street.

Perhaps less predictable is the number of industrial and commercial sites that are A-listed. These include:

The Govan Shipbuilders Offices and Store on Govan Road.

The Sentinel Works in Jessie Street, Polmadie, designed by
Archibald Leitch and Glasgow's first reinforced concrete
building.

The old fishmarket (the Briggait).

The former Prince's Dock Hydraulic Power Station on
Mavisbank Road.

Govan Graving Docks.

The Smith Mirrlees engineering works on West Street.

Arthur's Warehouse on Miller Street, Gardner's Warehouse
on Jamaica Street, (an iron-frame, concrete-clad warehouse
on McPhater Street in Cowcaddens, graded A for the very
advanced construction method), and a warehouse on Watson
Street featuring decoration borrowed from the style of
Alexander 'Greek' Thomson (see page 19).

The Templeton Carpet Factory by Glasgow Green.

The Scottish Ambulance Building on Milton Street.

The former North British Diesel Engine Works on South Street,
along with its 150-ton Titan Crane.

The Stobcross (Finnieston) Crane, the 175-ton giant cantilever
crane which is now a quayside icon.

Other less obvious A-listers are the open-air shelter at Bridgeton
Cross, the Horseshoe pub on Drury Street, Argyll Arcade including
Sloan's Café (the arcade was Scotland's earliest indoor shopping
mall, opened in 1824), the former Waverley cinema in Shawlands,
the former Hillhead picture house (now the Salon restaurant) and
the water tower of Ruchill Hospital.

Perhaps the most unusual A-listed structure in Glasgow is an
Edwardian multi-storey car park. When cars were new and
rare, parking on the street was illegal and undesirable, and for
city householders who did not have a stable or mews house
to convert into a garage, a public car park was essential. The
two-storey structure on Vinicombe Street in Hillhead was
purpose-built for the early motorists of the West End, and is
probably the earliest surviving example of a public garage in
Scotland.

Glasgow is a city where A-listed buildings often come in clusters, creating a collective urban landscape of exceptional architectural quality. One classic cluster is George Square, with the City Chambers, many of the surrounding buildings, the statues and even the lampbrackets. Other clusters can be found in the upmarket Park Circus development, and several West End terraces and streetscapes. In addition, dozens upon dozens of buildings on the principal city centre streets are A-listed, reflecting Glasgow's status as the country's leading centre of municipal and commercial Victorian architecture.

Another group within the A list features the former homes of Glasgow's commercial and industrial barons, such as Aikenhead House on Carmunnock Road, Redclyffe on Balgrayhill Road (designed by Charles Rennie Mackintosh), Tollcross House in Tollcross Park, Camphill House in Queen's Park, Craigie Hall in Dumbreck, and Woodbank on Partickhill Road.

Even more humble dwellings can be A-graded, such as 162–70 Gorbals Street (which incorporates the former British Linen Bank), the tall gushet Mercat Building on the London Road/Gallowgate junction, and even a tower block at Anniesland Court.

Almost thirty Glasgow churches are A-listed, as are all three of the city's cathedrals – Glasgow Cathedral, the Roman Catholic St Andrew's Cathedral on Clyde Street, and St Mary's Episcopal Cathedral on Great Western Road. Other A-listed religious buildings are the Hill Street Synagogue in Garnethill, and the Hindu Mandir on La Belle Place (formerly the Queen's Rooms).

Much of Glasgow University is A-listed, including the sixteenth-century Lion and Unicorn Staircase, and the entrance lodge, both of which were transported stone-by-stone from the university's original site in Townhead.

Other educational institutions similarly honoured are the Glasgow School of Art, the Martyrs' School, Notre Dame High School on Observatory Road, the former Scotland Street School, Kelvinside Academy, St Mungo's School Annexe on Duke Street, and Our Lady & St Francis Secondary School on Greendyke Street.

Public buildings that have achieved the highest architectural accolade number Langside Hall on Langside Avenue, Pollokshields Burgh Hall, part of the High Court, the former Sheriff Court on Ingram Street (now the Corinthian), the Pearce Institute in Govan, the Lodge of the Southern Necropolis and the Elder Park Library.

Elder Cottage Hospital, plus part of Leverndale Hospital, and the garden of the Gartnavel Royal Hospital, are all A-listed, as are the Theatre Royal, the King's Theatre, the Tron Theatre and the Mitchell Theatre.

Central station and the Central Hotel, along with the former St Enoch underground station on St Enoch Square, are both A-listed. The modernised Queen Street station itself is not A-listed, but the accolade is granted to its Victorian train shed and Cathedral Street Bridge.

The Nelson Monument and the Doulton Fountain in Glasgow Green, the statue of Mrs John Elder in Elder Park, the Lord Roberts Memorial and the Stewart Memorial Fountain in Kelvingrove Park, the equestrian statue of King William III near the cathedral and a cast iron fountain in Alexandra Park – all these are A-listed.

The most famous statue on the A list is that of the Duke of Wellington on Queen Street. The head of the equestrian sculpture is almost always fitted with a traffic cone – it even features that way in the opening credits of *Taggart*.

ALEXANDER 'GREEK' THOMSON

Charles Rennie Mackintosh aside (see page 158), Glasgow's most famous home-grown architect is Alexander Thomson (1817–85), known as 'Greek' Thomson for his use of design motifs from the ancient world. His most visible work is the enormous St Vincent Street church, which looks like a cross between a Greek temple and something out of ancient Egypt. It is a marker of Thomson's unique style.

Thomson's Caledonia Road church in Gorbals is now a fire-damaged shell, but a striking landmark nonetheless. His truly extraordinary Queen's Park church in Langside Road – which combined elements from Egypt, Greece and India – was destroyed by a German bomb in 1943.

Holmwood House in Cathcart, one of Thomson's best surviving works, is currently being renovated by the National Trust for Scotland – visitors can see the conservation work in progress.

Other works by Thomson – many of which are Grade A-listed – include:

The Buck's Head Building on Argyle Street, erected on the site of the famous Buck's Head Inn.
An office block on West Nile Street.
The lower part of the Grosvenor Building in Gordon Street.
The Grecian Chambers on the north side of Sauchiehall Street.
The warehouse and shops complex of the Egyptian Halls on Union Street.
'Castlehill' and 'Ellisland', a pair of suburban villas on Nithsdale Road.
'Maria Villa', a double villa on Mansionhouse Road in Langside.
The curved tenement block of Walmer Crescent, in Cessnock.
Thomson's own house on Moray Place in Strathbungo.

Thomson's gravestone is in the Southern Necropolis, a spooky black marble quasi-Egyptian structure installed in 2006 to replace the vandalised original.

CHURCHES

The design of the neo-Gothic Kelvinside Hillhead church on Saltoun Street was inspired by the thirteenth-century Sainte Chapelle in Paris.

The Barony North Church on Castle Street, aka the Evangelical Church, was inspired by the High Renaissance buildings of Rome, right down to the huge statues of the four evangelists on the balustrade.

The former Ramshorn Kirk on Ingram Street was the place of worship for many of the city's elite. Its superb Victorian stained-glass windows were put in storage at the start of both world wars. When the panels were last restored, just one error was made, with the texts for Abraham and Jacob wrongly interchanged – not bad for an astonishingly complex task involving thousands of separate pieces of coloured glass.

Govan Old Parish Church hosts one of the finest collections of Early Christian stones in Britain, dating from the tenth and eleventh centuries. There was originally a monastery on the site.

THE COUNCIL CHAMBERS

This grandiose Italian Renaissance building dominating George Square is arguably the apogee of Victorian municipal confidence. When the foundation stone was laid in 1883, 600,000 people attended the event or watched the associated parades – all helped by the declaration of an official city-wide holiday.

The Chambers took six years and £578,232 to build. When they were opened to the public in 1889, some 400,000 people visited over ten days.

In the late eighteenth century the land on which the Chambers were later to stand was sold by the council for £645, or 2s 8d per square yard. When the council bought it back in 1878, the asking price was £173,000, or £35 15s per square yard – so it was 268 times more expensive than the original sale.

Among the many names in the VIP visitors' book is that of Nelson Mandela, who received the Freedom of the City in 1993. A square nearby was renamed Nelson Mandela Place in his honour.

The exterior of the Chambers displays the standard measurements designed to ensure fair trading by everyone from shopkeepers to architects – so we have the standard inch, foot, two foot and yard. The 100ft measure, plus two now-archaic lengths, the chain and link, can be found by the North Lawn in George Square.

The Council Chambers are open for guided tours most weekdays. Go – the interiors are outstandingly elaborate.

THE GEORGE SQUARE STATUES

George Square, named for King George III, is a veritable forest of sculpture. Some are of very well-known figures:

Robert Burns (1759–96) – Scotland's national poet and author of 'Auld Lang Syne' and 'My Love Is Like A Red, Red Rose'.
Sir Walter Scott (1771–1832) – Scotland's most famous novelist.
James Watt (1736–1819) – inventor and mechanical engineer.
Queen Victoria (1819–1901) and Prince Albert (1819–61).
Sir Robert Peel (1788–1850) – Prime Minister 1834–5 and 1841–6.
William Ewart Gladstone (1809–98) – four times Prime Minister.

Robert Burns.

Thomas Campbell.

Others are less familiar to us modern folk:

Thomas Graham (1805–69) – chemistry pioneer at the University of Glasgow.
Thomas Campbell (1777–1844) – Scottish poet and historian.
Field Marshall Lord Clyde (Colin Campbell, 1792–1863) – famous Scottish soldier.
Sir John Moore (1761–1809) – hero of the Napoleonic Wars.
James Oswald MP (1779–1853) – supporter of the Reform Act of 1832, which expanded voting rights and transformed the political landscape of the nineteenth century.

The square also hosts:
The Commemorative Poverty Stone. This 1999 plaque includes an extract from the Declaration of Human Rights and states, 'poverty is neither inevitable nor acceptable.'

The Nagasaki Plaque, in memory of the victims of the atomic bombs dropped on Nagasaki and Hiroshima.

The Cenotaph, the city's principal war memorial, unveiled in 1924. The inscription reads: 'To the immortal honour of the officers, non-commissioned officers and men of Glasgow who fell in the Great War. This memorial is dedicated in proud and grateful recognition by the City of Glasgow.'

THE MARCH OF TIME

Until 1402 Lanarkshire included the whole of the Sheriffdom of Renfrew – what is now the County of Renfrewshire, home to Paisley, Johnstone, Gourock and Greenock.

Some of the retail stores in the Bath Street area have 'walkthroughs' from one street to another, which have to be legally retained as they are the imprints of the public rights of way that existed on the land before it was built over.

Sauchiehall Street was once a winding rural lane, lined with 'saughs' (willow trees). The 'hall' part of the name is a corruption of 'haugh', the Scots word for meadow.

Argyle Street was known as West Street until 1777. It is named after the Duke of Argyll, and historically has been spelt both 'Argyle' and 'Argyll', sometimes in the same document.

In 1906 the parliamentary constituency of Tradeston was created to represent Kingston, Tradeston and Kinning Park, the densely packed residents regularly sending a Labour MP to Westminster. The constituency vanished in the boundary changes of the 1950s. No prospective candidate would find much joy these days – Kingston and Tradeston have a permanent population hovering around zero.

LOST BURGHS

Glasgow Town Council became Glasgow Corporation in 1895, changing into the City of Glasgow District Council in 1975 and finally becoming Glasgow City Council twenty years later. Whatever the name, local government has always been a controversial subject in the area. As Glasgow changed and expanded it swallowed up neighbouring communities, including villages and burghs. A burgh was a self-organising unit of local government. The original Royal Burghs or Burghs of Baronry from the Middle Ages had the right to operate a market, control trade and raise taxes (Glasgow was a Burgh of Baronry). From the 1860s 'police burghs' tended to be developing urban areas, and had a town hall and their own police force, paid for from local taxes. Less well-organised areas were called districts. County councils did not appear until the end of the nineteenth century.

Here is the list of the casualties of Glasgow's appetite for expansion:

1846 – Gorbals. This annexation was partly prompted by the need to combine police forces so as to combat criminals on both sides of the river.

1891 – the 'great annexation'. The burghs of Hillhead, Maryhill, Pollokshields East, Pollokshields West, Crosshill, Govanhill, Kelvinside, Possilpark and Springburn were all absorbed, along with the districts of Langside, Shawlands and Mount Florida. At less than twelve years old (it was only created in 1879), Pollokshields East may have been the shortest-lived burgh in Scotland.

1905 – Kinning Park. This Lilliputian burgh was created in 1871, when it seceded from Govan. Tiny – less than 200 yards across at one point – it was the most densely populated burgh in Scotland, 14,000 people squeezing into just 100 acres.

1912 – the second great expansion. Govan, Partick, Pollokshaws, Anniesland, Temple, Scotstoun, Sheildhall, Shettleston, Tollcross and Cathcart all lost their independent status. The loss was deeply felt in the Burgh of Partick, with the provost handing over his chain of office and robe as a lament was played, and commenting, 'There they lie, the abandoned habits of the Provost of Partick, taken from him by Act of Parliament.' Govan, meanwhile, was the seventh most populous place in Scotland, and many Govanites thought Govan should have absorbed Glasgow, not the other way round.

1926 – the villages of Scotstounhill, Cardonald, Halfway and Crookston were annexed.

1975 – Rutherglen. Rutherglen was the oldest Royal Burgh in Scotland, and a bitter rival to the Johnny-come-lately Glasgow in the Middle Ages. Now it was just a suburb.

More recent boundary changes have relocated some of the places mentioned above into North or South Lanarkshire, or Renfrewshire, or East Dunbartonshire. These alterations to local government boundaries have magically reduced the City of Glasgow's population by a third, but the actual total for the metropolis of 'Greater Glasgow' – defined by urban area as distinct from boundaries – is still well over a million.

HOUSING

Glasgow's history of ultra-rapid industrial expansion and consequent immigration has made the provision of housing a political and financial hot potato since the nineteenth century – and into the present.

Glasgow is the UK capital of high-rise buildings. A pair of 31-floor blocks of flats on Bluevale Street and Whitevale Street in the East End are 290ft high, making them the tallest in Western Europe.

When the council transferred its housing stock in 2003, Glasgow Housing Association became the largest private landlord in Western Europe.

Many tower blocks built in the 1960s and '70s have recently been demolished, or are scheduled for destruction. When the Queen Elizabeth Square flats in Gorbals were taken down in 1993, debris from the explosion killed a local resident.

Tantallon Road in Shawlands was once home to the largest co-ownership development in Europe, a complex of flats, gardens and garages built in the 1970s.

Glasgow's first skyscraper was the Beresford Hotel, built on Sauchiehall Street for the 1938 Empire Exhibition. Despite changes of function, its Art Deco stylings can still be admired.

SOME STATISTICS ABOUT
GLASGOW'S ECONOMY
(WHICH ARE ACTUALLY QUITE INTERESTING)

Glaswegian annual economic output is worth around £15 billion. This is a result of 420,000 people currently being in work. This figure is 70,000 more than the city's post-war employment low-spot, which came in 1996. In 1935 Glasgow had 100,000 unemployed.

Half of all workers in the city commute in from other areas.

Between 1950 and 1990 the city's traditional manufacturing trades and heavy industries shrank by 90 per cent. Despite its industrial image, Glasgow is now overwhelmingly a service sector city. Financial and business services are the fastest-growing areas of the local economy.

UNIVERSITIES

Glasgow has three universities: the University of Glasgow (founded 1451); the University of Strathclyde (founded 1796); and Glasgow Caledonian University (founded 2007).

Between them the three universities, along with other institutions such as colleges and the Glasgow School of Art, host around 60,000 students.

For almost three centuries the University of Glasgow occupied the site of the former Blackfriars Monastery on High Street, before moving to the West End in 1870. The original location, having undergone many changes of use, is now partly occupied by a modern students' hall of residence.

In previous centuries the academic staff and students of the University of Glasgow were divided into four 'nations', according to their place of birth: *Glottiana* (Glasgow and Lanarkshire); *Rothseiana* (Ayrshire, Bute, Renfrewshire and the Clyde Coast); *Transforthiana* (the West and North of Scotland); and *Loudoniana*

(the Lothians and the Borders). The motto of the university is *Via, Veritas, Vita* – 'The Way, The Truth, The Life'.

The twin quadrangles of the University of Glasgow complex on Gilmorehill make up the second-largest neo-Gothic structure in Britain, after the Houses of Parliament.

Most older Scottish universities have a tradition of students voting for a rector every three years. The rector is an external figure who can be symbolic or proactive. In 2011 the former Liberal Democrat leader Charles Kennedy was re-elected as rector for his second consecutive term, the only person so honoured since Prime Minister Benjamin Disraeli in the 1870s.

Disraeli was one of eleven Prime Ministers to hold the rectorial post, including William Gladstone, Sir Robert Peel and Stanley Baldwin. In 1914, at the start of the First World War, the students, as a mark of solidarity with their allies, unanimously gave the rectorship to Raymond Poincaré, the President of France.

Other rectors whose election made a political point included Winnie Mandela (1987–90) and trade union leader Jimmy Reid (1971–4).

Some rectors have hailed from the world of popular culture, including Arthur Montford (tweed-jacketed presenter of *Scotsport*), television personality Johnny Ball, actor Richard Wilson, and soap star Ross Kemp (who was elbowed out after two years for not fulfilling his duties).

PARKS

Over 20 per cent of Glasgow's total land area is 'greenspace' – parkland, woodland, country areas and grassy open areas. This includes a grand total of 91 parks.

In 2007 Pollok Country Park was voted Britain's Best Park. The following year it won the award for Europe's Best Park.

Auchinlea Park received the Best Park in Scotland award in 2005. The following year the award was won by the Botanic Gardens, while Tollcross Park achieved the accolade in 2008.

Glasgow Green is Glasgow's oldest park, having been established in 1450. It has functioned as a common grazing ground, a linen-bleaching area, a sporting centre, a place for political rallies, and the site of the annual Glasgow fair and livestock mart.

Glasgow Green as it is known now was laid out between 1817 and 1826, with drainage and levelling to prevent the frequent flooding, and the channelling underground of the Camlachie and Molendinar burns.

On a fine Sunday in August 1894, 78,420 persons were counted as they entered Glasgow Green. There were no special events on – these were just visitors. Almost certainly the majority would have been working class people enjoying their day off in the nearest available open space.

Over the years plans were drawn up to sacrifice Glasgow Green to coal mining (early nineteenth century), railways (late nineteenth century) and a motorway (1960s). All such proposals have been successfully resisted.

Victoria Park in Scotstoun was not quite so lucky, losing a sizeable acreage to the approach roads for the Clyde Tunnel and Expressway.

Kelvingrove Park, landscaped between 1852 and 1867, was the first park in Scotland to be designed and constructed from scratch. It was originally known as the West End Park and was, from the get-go, a refined middle-class space.

Kelvingrove is rich in sculptures from the Victorian period to the present. The first piece installed was 'The Royal Bengal Tigress with a Peacock', created in Paris by Auguste Nicolas Caïn in 1867, and donated by John S. Kennedy, a New York millionaire who had emigrated from Glasgow.

Pollok Country Park has a herd of Highland cattle, and is the base for the mounted and dog-handling divisions of Strathclyde Police.

In the 1990s a protest camp dubbed the Pollok Free State was set up in an unsuccessful attempt to prevent the M77 motorway from slicing off part of Pollok Country Park. 5,000 trees were cut down for the road construction.

When the real estate for Queen's Park was purchased by the council in 1857, it was known as No Man's Land as it was in a disputed area between Renfrewshire, Govan and Glasgow.

Rosshall Park on Crookston Road has a secluded grotto built as the private swimming pool of the Cowan family, the original owners.

Cathkin Braes Country Park, south of Castlemilk, reaches 200 metres above sea level, making it the highest point in Glasgow.

The Medallion Garden in Auchinlea Park contains a 3-metre-tall specimen of the Giant Himalayan Lily.

Bellahouston Park has the most extensive collection of contemporary 'park art' in the city, as well as part of the ceremonial platform built for the Mass conducted by Pope John Paul II in 1982. 300,000 attendees, the largest public gathering ever seen in Scotland, sang 'Will Ye No Come Back Again?'

For those interested in horticultural history, the Botanic Gardens has a 'Chronological Border', which gives the dates when popular garden plants were first introduced to Britain, starting with the sixteenth century. The only other similar border in the UK is in the Botanic Gardens at Cambridge University.

Tollcross Park used to have a herd of deer, introduced to give city dwellers a taste of the Scottish natural heritage that was famous worldwide, but completely unknown to most working-class Glaswegians.

The Scottish Poetry Rose Garden in Queen's Park is a unique site that features verses praising roses by twelve Scottish poets, from Robert Burns to Sorley McLean.

One of Glasgow's most recent green spaces was created in 2005. Beardmore Park was landscaped out of derelict land in the East End, between Shettleston Road and Westmuir Street, Parkhead.

MINES

Glasgow's industrial might was enabled by the vast reserves of natural resources in the immediate area. Mines were everywhere. The Romans worked the lead mines of Lanarkshire and gold from the area was being collected in the Middle Ages. Later centuries saw the mass exploitation of blackband ironstone, limestone, sandstone, fire-clay, and ordinary clay for making bricks.

Mining for coal had been known around Paisley since the twelfth century. By the sixteenth century coal was being worked in Craigton, Drumoyne and Cambuslang, as well as many other places. In 1908 Lanarkshire produced over 17 million tons of coal, making it the most productive county in Scotland.

There was once a coal mine in George Square and another at the top of Langside Road near Queen's Park. A horizontal adit near Baldernock was accessed from behind a waterfall.

Up until 1799 all the miners in the Cambuslang pits were *de facto* slaves, the property of the mineowner, the Duke of Hamilton. Men who dared to leave the job could be charged with theft and vagrancy, because they had 'stolen' themselves from their master. Boys who were not strong enough for the coalface work were sold to the duke's cronies as servants.

Mick McGahey (1925–99), the leader of the Scottish miners during some of the industry's most testing times, worked in the Cambuslang pits. A memorial to him stands on Main Street.

On 15 March 1851 the Victoria pit of Nitshill colliery became the site of Scotland's worst mining disaster when sixty-one men and boys died in an explosion. A belated commemoration sculpture was erected next to Nitshill war memorial.

FIRES

Early Glasgow was a crowded community of mostly wooden buildings; fires were inevitably all too common.

A chronicle from 1652 describes the great fire of 17 July on that year:

> It pleased God to lay the town of Glasgow desolate by a violent and sudden fire. The far best part of the four streets and most considerable buildings were burnt, together with above fourscore lanes and closes, which were the dwellings of above a thousand families, and almost all the shops and warehouses of the merchants, many whereof are near by ruined. Besides, a great many more of widows, orphans, and distressed honest families, having lost what they had, are now put to starving and begging. The like of this fire has not been formerly heard of in this nation.

Glasgow Cross, Saltmarket, Trongate and Bridgegate were all destroyed, 1,060 houses being burnt.

The second great fire took place in 1677, wiping out most of Saltmarket and the Cross, and making between 600 and 700 families homeless.

Clearly the 1677 blaze overwhelmed the city's first fire engine, purchased by the magistrates two decades earlier. A second fire engine was finally obtained in 1725, at a cost of £50 and brought all the way from London.

The one positive aspect of the 1677 conflagration was that new building regulations were enforced, widening streets and discouraging timber houses with thatched roofs. A third city-wide fire in 1684, although serious, was therefore not quite so devastating.

Modern Glasgow suffered major fires in 1951, 1960 and 1968, but the worst peacetime blaze took place on 28 March 1961, when fourteen firefighters and five members of Glasgow Salvage Corps were killed during the Cheapside Street disaster. The inferno consumed a bonded warehouse in Anderston containing 1,043,088 gallons of whisky and 31,107 gallons of rum, and then spread to adjacent premises. The streets were rivers of burning alcohol. Six members of Glasgow Fire Service received bravery awards. There are memorials in the Necropolis and close to Cheapside Street.

EMBASSIES AND CONSULATES

There are no embassies in Glasgow (or elsewhere in Scotland) but the city does host consulates from:

Denmark
Germany
India
The Netherlands
Norway
Pakistan
Rwanda
Thailand
Tunisia

GLASGOWS OVERSEAS

With so many Scottish emigrants seeking new horizons over the centuries, it is not surprising there are many Glasgows (or related names) in the wider world (although to be strictly accurate, some of them were named after settlers with the surname Glasgow).

Australia
Kelvin Grove, Queensland, is a suburb of Brisbane.

Rutherglen, Victoria, is a small community near the Murray River.

Canada

New Glasgow in Nova Scotia has a population of 9,455.

The province of Ontario has a Glasgow, a New Glasgow, and a Port Glasgow. Scarborough, an area in the Ontario capital Toronto, was previously known as Glasgow in the eighteenth century.

Glasgow Island is an uninhabited island off Baffin Island, while New Glasgow is an empty area on Prince Edward Island.

Jamaica

The Caribbean island has one small village, near the west coast, and two smaller places, near Montego Bay and Morant Bay, all named Glasgow.

USA

There are numerous Glasgows in the USA. By size of population they are:

Glasgow, Kentucky (population 14,200)
Glasgow, Delaware (population 12,840)
Glasgow, Iowa (population 12,434)
Glasgow Village, Missouri (population 5,234)
Glasgow, Montana (population 3,253)
Glasgow, Missouri (population 1,263) – the Battle of Glasgow
    was fought here in 1864 during the American Civil War
Glasgow, Virginia (population 1,046)
Glasgow, West Virginia (population 783)
Glasgow Township, Minnesota (population 298)
Glasgow, Illinois (population 170)
Glasgow, in Fallen Timber County, Pennsylvania (population 63)

Glasgow Village is a district of Pottstown, Pennsylvania. Glasgow Cemetery is in Thomas County, Georgia. Glasgow Landing is a jetty in South Carolina. Glasgow, California, is an empty spot beside the highway in the Mojave Desert. The Glasgow in Coos County, Oregon, is a store with a self-proclaimed mayor (who is also the sheriff and dog catcher).

Glasgow is also the name of a historic home (built 1792) in Cambridge, Maryland. There are buildings called Glasgow in Butler County, Alabama and Columbiana, Ohio.

Glasgow, in Renault Monroe County, Illinois, vanished as a place-name in the 1870s. The Glasgows in Black Hawk County, Iowa, and Weakley County, Tennessee, have also disappeared. The Glasgow in Tuscarawas County, Ohio, appears to have been absorbed by its neighbours.

A miniature book on the Glasgows of America was published by the Conclave of the Miniature Book Society, which was held in Glasgow in 1990.

Suriname
This tropical South American country has a Glasgow with a population of 776.

TWIN TOWNS

Glasgow is twinned with the following cities:

Nuremberg, Germany
Turin, Italy
Marseilles, France
Lahore, Pakistan
Rostov-on-Don, Russia
Dalian, China
Havana, Cuba
Bethlehem, Palestine

In addition the city has a formal technical partnership with Amathole District Municipality in South Africa, and a development project with Malawi.

THE WATCHERS ON THE WALLS

Glasgow is one of the champion cities for Victorian and Edwardian gargoyles and other sculptures. There are literally thousands of statues, grotesques and other figures, with the greatest concentrations in the city centre and the West End.

Common elements include St Mungo's Bell, Trees, Birds and Fish, some of which appear in crossword puzzle-like complexity.

An insurance company's building on Bothwell Street spells out the owners' name using symbols – a lion rampant *(Scottish)*, a judge's wig *(Legal)*, a fountain *(Life)* and a castle *(Assurance)*.

In mythology, griffons were guardians of treasure; it is therefore not surprising to find them hovering protectively above the Stock Exchange on Nelson Mandela Place.

The former Sheriff Court on Wilson Street has a long frieze depicting a trial by jury, complete with the murder victim, and the accused held in chains. The jury are all wearing togas.

Brechin's Bar on Govan Road has a cat carved on its façade. There are several stories that attempt to explain it, but its real origin is a mystery.

If you get out your binoculars and study the Victorian spire of St Mary's Episcopal Cathedral on Great Western Road, you can spot a tiny lancet window with a modern boss carved in the form of a kestrel. The bird nested in the space in the early 1990s, delaying the restoration builders by several weeks.

Other unusual sculptures to look out for are an Egyptian Pharaoh and a Native American chief (Bothwell Street); a bust of Beethoven (Renfrew Street); Pan, the Greek god of nature (Bellgrove Street); the Statue of Liberty (Queen's Drive); a miniature Viking longboat (St Vincent Place) and a pair of bewigged judges (Hope Street).

In 2002 a suspended bronze figure called The Gatekeeper developed a reddish stain on the palm of its outstretched hand, similar to the marks of the wounds of Christ exhibited by stigmatics. Inevitably the phenomenon attracted quasi-religious or spiritual interpretations, and the sculpture on Caledonia Road was dubbed 'The Angel' (despite not having any wings). The sculpture's creator, artist Matt Baker, thought that a steel pin had accidentally been left in the hand, and had become rusted by dripping water. The stain has now almost entirely vanished.

SOME COMMON GLASWEGIAN URBAN MYTHS

Myth: An entire street, complete with shops and houses, lies beneath Central station.

Reality: The village of Grahamston was indeed swept away when the station was built, but nothing remains. There is no secret subterranean street.

Myth: The statue of Sir Walter Scott in George Square was carved with the plaid over the wrong shoulder, which led to shame and disgrace for the sculptor.

Reality: The location of the plaid on the right shoulder conforms to the usual convention for Borderers, of which Scott was one; only Highlanders were depicted with the plaid on the left shoulder.

Myth: The Kelvingrove Art Gallery and Museum was built back-to-front; when the architect found out, he killed himself by jumping off the roof.

Reality: The museum was erected, perfectly correctly, on its current orientation for the Great Exhibition of 1901. The removal of the temporary buildings gave some the illusion that the 'front' was the 'back'. As for the architect's mistake-driven suicide, this is a myth propagated in many cities in Europe and America – none of the stories are true.

Myth: The Tait Tower, part of the 1938 Empire Exhibition, was demolished to prevent it becoming a landmark for German bombers.

Reality: The 300ft high steel 'Tower of the Empire', like most of the temporary buildings in Bellahouston Park, was simply removed after the exhibition closed. Other landmarks of similar height, such as the University of Glasgow's Gilmorehill tower, were not demolished.

Myth: A piper and his dog suffered a mysterious fate in a secret tunnel between the cathedral and the old kirk of Rutherglen; the pipes could be heard from above ground until they were extinguished by an evil monster, or the devil.

Reality: No such subterranean passage ever existed. The story of the ill-fated piper and his dog (with the latter usually escaping, although hairless and injured) is a well-worn supernatural folktale found throughout Scotland – over twenty separate examples have been recorded, from Edinburgh to Skye.

Myth: A man urinated on the live electric cable in one of the subway stations, and was instantly vaporised, leaving only his boots melted to the platform.

Reality: This story was deliberately propagated in the 1960s by a group of students; variants can be found from cities all over the world.

2

THE RIVER CLYDE & OTHER WATERWAYS

THE CHANGING CLYDE

The full length of the river is some 106 miles, the last 20 of which are in the basin occupied by Glasgow and the Clyde Estuary.

During prehistoric times the Clyde was much higher than it is today, its broad estuary covering what is now Glasgow, Johnstone and Paisley. Several Neolithic wooden canoes have been found far above present-day water levels.

By the time the Romans were building the Antonine Wall between the Forth and the Clyde (AD 142), the river level had fallen to roughly what it is today.

As a potential water highway the Clyde had a severe problem: it was choked with islands and sandbanks, and parts of the river were shallow enough to walk across at low tide. Only the smallest boats could make it as far as Glasgow, and even they were entirely dependent on the tide. It took several hundred years to make the river fit for shipping.

In the sixteenth century an attempt was made to improve the channel at Dumbuck, between Glasgow and Dumbarton, but it failed.

A map of 1654 shows six permanent islands between Glasgow Bridge and Renfrew, and there were more downriver, plus numerous shoals and sandbanks. Two of the islands, Whiteinch and King's Inch, are still places on the north and south sides of the river respectively, having been joined to the shore.

In the 1660s a coal-owner from Gorbals complained that he could not load his ships at the Broomielaw 'from the scarcity of water'.

In 1668 the magistrates of Glasgow, desperate for an improvement in trade, bowed to the inevitable and purchased land at the mouth of the Firth of Clyde, eventually creating Port Glasgow. Ships unloaded here and the goods were either taken many miles by pack-horses along dreadful roads to Glasgow, or transported upriver on shallow-draft vessels called lighters.

In 1769 James Watt surveyed the river and found that the water at the ¼-mile-long Hirst shoal (between the Broomielaw and Anderston) was just 14in deep at low tide. Even at high water it was only 3ft 3in in depth.

In 1770 John Golborne of Chester started dredging and constructing jetties. After five years of work, parts of the river were 7ft deep. Further improvements, assisted by the new steam-driven dredgers, cleared channels, removed sandbanks and shoals, and continued to deepen the riverbed.

The Clyde froze over for three months during the winter of 1784/5.

The Elderslie Rock, a massive volcanic plug extending right across the river about 8ft below low water, was a major hazard to shipping. In 1854 it holed the steamship SS *Glasgow* on its voyage to New York. It took £140,000 and 25 years of blasting to finally remove the rock.

By the mid-nineteenth century, and after vast expenditure and labour, the broad, shallow and hazardous estuary was now one of the major seaways of the world, bringing thousands of large ocean-going vessels into the heart of Glasgow. As the saying goes, 'Glasgow made the Clyde and the Clyde made Glasgow'.

THE HARBOUR

The first appearance of anything approaching a harbour in Glasgow was not until 1662, when a small stone-built quay, along with a crane and weigh-house, was erected on the rural riverside at Broomielaw. Only the smallest of vessels, carrying from 3 to 6 tons, with a draft shallow enough to cope with the low water, could make it this far upriver.

Extensions were made to the harbour in 1722, 1792 and 1811.

In 1891 there were 4 miles of quays on the north side of the river, and a further 2 miles on the opposite bank.

In 1656, twelve vessels were sailing to and from Glasgow, carrying 957 tons over their year's journeys. In 1891 some 20,000 vessels arrived a year, carrying more than 4 million tons of goods.

The Glasgow College of Nautical Studies on Adelphi Street currently teaches one third of all merchant maritime trainees in the UK. Up until the mid-twentieth century the school was regarded as a kind of land-based ship, and so, in keeping with tradition, female staff – thought to be unlucky on a sea-going vessel – were confined to an annexe.

THE RIVER ENVIRONMENT

The physical consequences of the river improvements have been immense. In 1912 the title-deeds of some Renfrew houses still gave the Clyde as the boundary of their gardens, even though the town was now more than a ½ mile from the riverside.

Glasgow's vast concentration of factories and people meant that the river, once famed for its salmon, became little more than a lifeless industrial sewer. In the People's Palace Museum is a bottle of water collected from the Clyde in 1893: it is pitch black.

After an extensive campaign, salmon finally returned to the river in the 1990s, but the 'dead water' of the dredged area in the estuary is now so deep it does not contain enough oxygen for all of the migrating fish to survive.

Three clean-up boats now patrol the river for litter.

The Clyde Walkway, a UK National Trail opened in 2005, runs for 40 miles along the north bank of the river from Partick, through the city centre and Glasgow Green and then to Cambuslang and eventually New Lanark.

FLOODS

In 1712 the Clyde flooded, trapping 1,200 families in the upper parts of their houses, drowning several people, and allowing a boat to be sailed along Bridgegate.

In the 1720s Daniel Defoe visited Glasgow twice. The first time he crossed the Clyde next to Glasgow Bridge, the trickle barely coming over his horse's hooves. On the next occasion the town was flooded and the waters were threatening to sweep the bridge away.

In recent years there have been severe floods in 1936 and 2002.

SAVING THE DROWNED

With an unpredictable river that swung from a footwash to a flood, and bathing a popular pastime, it was not surprising that drownings were common.

In the nineteenth century a ferryload of millworkers overturned. Many of the desperate survivors clung to a strong swimmer named James Lambert. Unable to swim with his burden he sank to the bottom several times and 'bounced' off the riverbed until he could reach the shore. In all he rescued about twenty people that day, and went on to save around sixty more during his lifetime. His last rescue cost him his eyesight.

The Glasgow Humane Society was set up in 1790 to rescue people from the Clyde. It was founded by the Faculty of Physicians and Surgeons of Glasgow via a bequest of £200 from a wealthy merchant.

Rescue apparatus was kept at Glasgow Green. The first Humane Society House was erected on the Green in 1795. It successor, Society's House, is still there.

For more than 200 years the society's officers have come from only two families, Geddes and Parsonage. George Geddes I was officer from 1859 to 1889 and George Geddes II officer from 1878 to 1928. George Geddes II's son, also called George, drowned during a rescue in 1929. Ben Parsonage BEM was officer from 1932 until his death in 1979. Over the last forty years the current officer, George Parsonage MBE, has rescued over 1,000 people, and recovered hundreds of bodies.

FORDS

The earliest known crossing points were a pair of fords roughly where the Albert Bridge stands now, at the bottom of Saltmarket.

Another medieval crossing point was Marlin Ford near Renfrew. At high tide a raft was brought into use. In the opposite direction, there was a ford at Dalmarnock.

Until 1768 it was possible to cross at low tide from Govan using a set of stepping stones.

A crossing point near Cambuslang was known as the 'Thief's Ford' or the 'Flier's Ford' and, according to tradition, was where Mary, Queen of Scots crossed the river in her flight south after the Battle of Langside (1568).

BRIDGES AND TUNNELS

The first timber bridge dates from around 1285. The first stone bridge was built on the same site by Bishop Rae in 1345, at the bottom of what is now Bridgegate and Stockwell Street, thus linking the route from the south to the High Street and the cathedral.

In the same way that the later dredging of the Clyde made industrial Glasgow possible, so Bishop Rae's bridge virtually created medieval Glasgow as an important centre of commerce. On the south bank a small village grew up called Bridgend – later to become Gorbals.

For centuries Glasgow Bridge was the most westerly permanent crossing on the Clyde, its nearest rival being Bothwell Bridge some 10 miles upriver. The bridge ensured the upstart town of Glasgow outstripped older burghs such as Rutherglen (the latter is now a suburb of Glasgow). After 600 years of service, Glasgow Bridge was removed in the nineteenth century.

The bridges and tunnels crossing the Clyde in Glasgow, from east to west, are:

Dalmarnock Bridge, linking Rutherglen and Dalmarnock. It was opened in 1891, replacing timber predecessors from 1821 and 1848, which in turn had superseded the Farme Ford.

Dalmarnock Railway Bridge, which carries the suburban line to Dalmarnock and Bridgeton. Completed in 1897, it replaced its 1861 predecessor, the piers of which can be seen immediately to the west.

Rutherglen Bridge, linking Dalmarnock and Shawfield. Built in 1896, it replaced a narrow hog-backed predecessor constructed in 1775 by James Watt. The Victorian piers had to be dug 60ft through soft sand and silt until solid bedrock was reached.

Polmadie Bridge, a footbridge linking Provost Way with the playing fields on the north bank. It was built in 1955.

King's Bridge, running between Gorbals and Bridgeton, is so flat and wide drivers may not notice they are crossing a river.

St Andrew's Suspension Bridge, which takes pedestrians from Adelphi Street to Glasgow Green. A masterpiece of attractive Victorian heritage built in 1856 and now painted a suitable St Andrew's blue, it replaced a ferry that was becoming increasingly dangerous for the hordes of factory workers.

Pipe Bridge and Weir. No crossing here, but the weir and the huge pipes above it are a striking sight.

Albert Bridge (the A8) between Saltmarket and Gorbals. Erected in 1871 and formerly known as the Hutchesontown Bridge, this is the fifth structure on the site. The first, begun in 1794, was swept away by a flood a year later.

City Union Railway Bridge (disused). In 1870 the first railway bridge across the Clyde was opened here. It proved inadequate to cope with the traffic to St Enoch station so a second tier was built above it in 1899. This second bridge was the first of the permanent Clyde bridges to have a steel superstructure. St Enoch station is no more, and the railway bridge now supports a fine selection of vegetation.

Victoria Bridge (also the A8) between Stockwell Street and Gorbals. This is on the site of the very first Clyde bridges of 1285 and 1345, and thus can be said to be a key node in medieval Glasgow. Opened in 1854, the Victoria Bridge is Glasgow's oldest surviving complete Clyde bridge.

South Portland Suspension Bridge. This pedestrian crossing, with its striking triumphal arch towers, was built in 1853, replacing an earlier wooden bridge.

The twin Glasgow Subway tunnels between St Enoch and Bridge Street stations.

Glasgow Bridge (usually called Jamaica Street Bridge or, before that, the Broomielaw Bridge), the A77 from Eglinton over to

Jamaica Street. The first bridge on this site, erected in 1772, had approaches so steep that horse-drawn vehicles struggled to ascend. Its replacement was built by Thomas Telford in the 1830s. The present structure, opened in 1899, was by popular demand based on Telford's design. The caissons are sunk 100ft into the silt to sit on the bedrock.

The first Caledonian Railway Bridge, built in 1879 and dismantled in the 1960s. On the remaining rusticated granite piers are incised the lines 'ALL GREATNESS STANDS FIRM IN THE STORM' in English and Greek, a reference from Plato's *Republic*. The artwork was created as part of a 1990 arts competition and was suggested by the poet Ian Hamilton Finlay. There is no plaque attributing the work to Finlay, and he received no artist's fee for the project.

The second Caledonian Railway Bridge, built immediately east of the earlier bridge in 1905, and now the main railway bridge to Glasgow Central. At one point it was the widest river-crossing railway bridge in Britain.

George V Bridge (also the A77), connecting the south side with Broomielaw. It opened in 1928 having been long delayed by the First World War.

Tradeston Bridge, often called the 'Squiggly Bridge' because of its distinctive double-curved 'S' shape. This pedestrian route is the newest of Glasgow's bridges, opening in 2009 to link the developing Tradeston area with the pride-of-the-city International Financial Services District.

The Kingston Bridge, the notoriously queue-prone M8 crossing, opened in 1970. At the time it was the longest pre-stressed concrete bridge in Scotland, and the second longest in Britain. 170,000 vehicles use its ten lanes every day, making it at peak times one of the busiest sections of road in Europe.

Glasgow Harbour Tunnel (closed). Built in the 1890s between Tunnel Street in Finnieston and Mavisbank Quay, the vehicle and pedestrian tunnels have been completely sealed since the 1980s.

Their positions are marked by the distinctive rotunda buildings on either side of the river.

The Clyde Arc or Finnieston Bridge, a graceful 2006 structure with a bowstring arch, linking Govan and Finnieston. It is sometimes called the 'Squinty Bridge' because it crosses the river at a sharp angle.

Bell's Bridge, erected in 1988 to allow pedestrians access between the Scottish Exhibition & Conference Centre and the site of the then Glasgow Garden Festival.

The Millennium Bridge, opened in 2002 and linked to the Glasgow Science Centre development. Like Bell's Bridge, part of it can be opened to allow the passage of larger vessels. These two pedestrian crossings now link the new Govan and its media and technology 'village' with the SECC and the major hotels on the north bank.

The twin Glasgow Subway tunnels under the river between Partick and Govan stations.

The Clyde Tunnel, a thundering expressway linking the Clydeside Expressway with Linthouse, Shieldhall and the M8 south of the river. Opened in 1963 with an estimated daily use of 13,000 vehicles, the current traffic is around 65,000 vehicles per day. The river is 123m wide at this point, the tunnels being more than 760m long. There is also a subway for pedestrians and cycles running alongside each of the paired tunnels.

There is no further crossing (with the exception of the Renfrew–Yoker pedestrian ferry) until the high-level Erskine Bridge linking Paisley and the M8 with Clydebank.

St Andrews Suspension Bridge, South Portland Suspension Bridge, Albert Bridge and Victoria Bridge are all A-listed, meaning they are architectural structures of national or international importance.

THE MOLENDINAR BURN

Glasgow was not actually founded on the Clyde, but on the banks of the Molendinar Burn, which was the stream next to the cathedral and the medieval town clustering at the top of High Street. It rises from Hogganfield Loch, off Cumbernauld Road near Stepps.

As well as a source of fresh water, the Molendinar was later used to power a series of meal and flour mills. Its name derives from *molen,* an old word for mill.

In the seventeenth century owners of properties on the Saltmarket had the right to fish in the burn.

As the city developed the burn became increasingly polluted and built over. Although now almost entirely vanished from sight, it is still there, running through a brick-lined Victorian culvert buried beneath Wishart Street, the Tennents Brewery and the High Court, and then down to the Clyde.

A tiny open stretch can be seen next to the old Great Eastern Hotel on Duke Street.

THE RIVER KELVIN

The Kelvin is Glasgow's second river, a 22-mile meander from the moors near Kilsyth through Bardowie, Maryhill and the West End, entering the Clyde at Yorkhill Basin.

Unlike the Molendinar, many people are familiar with the Kelvin because it flows in the open, through Maryhill, the Botanic Gardens and Kelvingrove Park and past the University of Glasgow. Riverside walks are popular, as is the Kelvin Cycle Way from Partick to Summerston.

As with the Molendinar, the Kelvin was formerly used to power watermills. The river became badly polluted and litter-strewn, and its current cleaner state is in large part due to the efforts of FORK, Friends of the River Kelvin. Salmon have now returned to the river.

For much of its length the river is close to the Forth and Clyde Canal, and in places is used as an overflow for the canal. At Maryhill the Kelvin Aqueduct carries the canal over the river.

One of the Kelvin's tributaries is the Allander Water, which runs through Milngavie.

Several significant and traffic-heavy bridges cross the river in the West End, including Queen Margaret Bridge beside the Botanic Gardens, the Great Western Bridge on Great Western Road (which is A-listed), Partick Bridge on Dumbarton Road, and the Clydeside Expressway. The bridge on Kelvin Way has some of the best public sculpture in Glasgow.

The Kelvin has given its name to Kelvindale, Kelvinbridge, Kelvingrove and Kelvinhaugh, not to mention Kelvin Hall. When the great scientist Wiliam Thomson was ennobled, he took the title Lord Kelvin.

THE WHITE CART WATER AND BLACK CART WATER

These two rivers join close to Glasgow Airport before decanting into the Clyde between Renfrew and Erskine. The low-lying semi-island they create between them provided the ideal level ground for an airport.

The White Cart rises among the moors of Eaglesham and flows for 26 miles through Busby, Linn Park, Cathcart, Langside, Pollokshaws, Pollok Country Park and Crookston to Paisley.

The monks of Paisley Abbey took timber and coal from the Clyde up the Cart to the centre of Paisley. The river was rich in salmon and trout at this time.

As with the Molendinar and the Kelvin, the two Carts were harnessed to drive several mills. Dripps Mill in Waterfoot, on the White Cart south of Clarkston, still has a pair of working nineteenth-century waterwheels.

The White Cart is crossed by numerous bridges, the most interesting of which is the Swing Bridge, built in 1923 west of Renfrew. The original swing bridge was erected in 1838. A moving bridge was required here because the river is navigable by ships as far as Paisley. The two parts move upwards as in a drawbridge, so strictly it is not a swing bridge but a bascule bridge.

Paisley used to be a shipbuilding centre and in the mid-nineteenth century was celebrated for constructing the swiftest river steamers then operating on the Clyde.

As with the other rivers in the area, the White Cart became abominably polluted in the nineteenth century. At one point Paisley had the reputation of being the filthiest town in Britain.

The White Cart has flooded parts of south Glasgow more than twenty times since 1908. In 1984 Battlefield and Langside were inundated when water levels in the river rose by more than a metre an hour. Major flood prevention works are underway.

The Black Cart is a less energetic river than its partner; on its route from Castle Semple Loch via Johnstone it falls less than 90ft over 10 miles, and hence can be quite sluggish.

The White Cart Way is a 4-mile walk between Pollok Park and Linn Park, via Pollokshaws, Shawlands, Newlands, Langside and Cathcart, passing Pollok House and the National Trust for Scotland property of Holmwood House.

It has been speculated that the White Cart, linking as it does several parks and patches of countryside, may provide a 'green corridor' for the 'big cats' that have been reported in an arc from Linn Park through south-west Glasgow to Johnstone and Paisley.

3

WARS, BATTLES & RIOTS

LOST IN THE MISTS OF TIME

King Arthur in Glasgow? Perhaps. Some scholars think that the sixth of Arthur's twelve battles, as described in the ninth-century work *Historia Brittonum* by Nennius, took place near Cambuslang in about AD 508.

MEDIEVAL MAYHEM

We're on more solid ground with the Battle of Renfew from 1164, when Malcolm IV, King of Scots, defeated Somerled, the Lord of the Isles. According to one report the Gaelic warlord brought 160 galleys to the fight, but both he and his son were slain and the Islesmen suffered a great setback in their attempt to make Scotland a Gaelic kingdom.

A Glasgow monk named William claimed to have witnessed the slaughter, and attributed the victory of the Scots to the miraculous intervention of St Kentigern. Somerled's severed head was handed over to Bishop Herbert at Glasgow Cathedral, and displayed as proof that the saint's spirit had joined in the fray on behalf of the Lowland Scots.

WILLIAM WALLACE

According to the dubious chronicler Blind Harry, William Wallace took the Bishop's Castle from the English in about 1300, attacking on two fronts, up High Street and along Drygate. The 'Battle of the Bell o' the Brae' may or may not have happened but Blind Harry's idea that the small castle had a garrison of 1,000 men is just ridiculous – 50 would be more likely. The numbers were presumably exaggerated to make Wallace's victory more impressive.

The Ratton Well on Stockwell Street had a foul taste. This was supposed to have derived from Mr Wallace throwing the dead bodies of the English troops down the well, while saying 'Stock it well, lads, stock it well.' This silly story makes the inflated garrison numbers look positively sensible.

Again according to tradition, it was during a meeting at Rutherglen church that Scottish nobleman Sir John Menteith was persuaded to betray the hero of the War of Independence. Wallace was captured close to Robroyston in 1305.

THE WARS OF MARY, QUEEN OF SCOTS

In 1544 the Earl of Arran, the Regent (the ruler of Scotland while Mary was underage), defeated the rebel Earl of Lennox at the Battle of the Butts, on Gallowmuir on the north side of Gallowgate. Around 300 of Lennox's troops and citizens of Glasgow were killed.

One of the slain was named by the historian Hollinshed as the Baron of Argentine. Nothing to do with South America, this was a simple mistranslation of the Latin rendering of the title of the Laird of Silvertonhill – the Latin for silver is *argent*.

Also in 1544 some of Lennox's forces were besieged in the Bishop's Castle. After ten days they surrendered upon being promised safe passage. As soon as the gates were opened the treacherous Earl of

Arran had all of the garrison executed, only two men escaping the slaughter.

A lion-topped column on Battlefield Road marks the site of the Battle of Langside where, in 1568, Mary, Queen of Scots was defeated by her half-brother the Earl of Moray. In less than an hour some 300 of Mary's troops were killed. They are reputed to be buried in the area of Queen's Park, which was itself named after Mary. The defeated queen fled to England, to become the permanent prisoner-guest of Elizabeth I.

In 1570 – with the Earl of Moray assassinated – a party of Mary's supporters besieged the Bishop's Castle. The garrison of twenty-four men successfully defended their position and the siege was abandoned.

Two years later the shop-keepers and tradesmen of Glasgow were required by law to take to the road to supply the Scots army. They were compelled 'to follow the army where it shall repair, with bread, ale, and all other kinds of vivers for men and horse, which shall be bought from them with ready money and thankful payment.'

THE COVENANTERS AND THE CIVIL WARS

By and large the major campaigns of the seventeenth and eighteenth centuries passed Glasgow by, as the city was not on the usual marching routes for armies. Glasgow never had a town wall or a strong defensible position, and once the Bishop's Castle fell into disrepair any conflicts tended to take place on the edge of the city. A good example was the Battle of Kilsyth in 1645, when the Marquis of Montrose's army killed thousands of Covenanters. This outcome led Glasgow to surrender to the Royalists.

In 1679 a group of Covenanters attacked the celebrations being held in Rutherglen to mark the restoration of Charles II. A group of dragoons under Viscount Dundee, Graham of Claverhouse, set off from Glasgow and were given a bloody nose by the Covenanters at the Battle of Drumclog in south Lanarkshire. This was the only battle the redoubtable Claverhouse ever lost. He retreated to Glasgow, raised barricades across High Street, Gallowgate and Saltmarket, and smacked the Covenanters down in a brief skirmish, killing eight.

Later that year a Royalist army trounced the Covenanters at the Battle of Bothwell Brig near Hamilton. Once the dust had settled the treasurer of Glasgow Council promptly presented the victors with a bill for £3,211, covering expenses and provisions for the soldiers and their horses and baggage, and for 'entertaining the lord general [Claverhouse] when he came to this burgh and the rest of the noblemen and gentlemen with him.' Clearly there was no such thing as a free lunch in Glasgow.

PIRATES OF THE CLYDE

A war with Holland between 1665 and 1667 saw entrepreneurial Glasgow merchants fitting out ships to attack Dutch merchantmen and steal their cargos – in other words, piracy. One such privateer brought home not only a merchant ship laden with valuable salt, but also a small Dutch gunboat. The size of the prize meant that Captain Chambers and his backers in the Glasgow business community were quids in.

THE JACOBITE WARS

In 1685 the Presbyterian Earl of Argyll raised an ineffective rebellion against the Catholic King James II (VII of Scotland). Blocked at Old Kilpatrick, Argyll fled across the Clyde and was captured near Inchinnan. The stone where he rested is still called the Argyll Stone and is supposedly streaked red with the blood from his wounds. It is actually an early medieval cross-base.

During the first Jacobite rebellion of 1689–90 the government wished to build a fort at Inverlochy in the West Highlands. Glasgow was called upon to provide all the supply ships and construction materials, as well as 500 spades, shovels, and pick-axes. The bill was promptly presented to the army.

Loyalist-minded Glasgow played no direct part in the 1715 Jacobite Rebellion, although protective barricades and trenches were constructed at several points including Gallowgate, Cowloan and Rottenrow, and a shipment of rebel guns destined for the Highlands was seized on a boat at Broomielaw. As usual, the most detailed records of the period deal with how much everything cost – in preparing to defend their city, and in sustaining the many rebel prisoners kept in Glasgow, the council spent the huge sum of £12,078 (Scots), 8s and 10d. This included 58s for cabbages and leeks 'destroyed by the trenches', and £116 'for transporting the great guns'.

Glasgow played no military part in the 1745 rebellion, the burgesses considering that destruction and war damage was bad for business. But what did attract the Jacobites was the city's growing wealth.

In September 1745, when he was occupying Edinburgh and was effectively the master of Scotland, Bonnie Prince Charlie sent a demand to the magistrates of Glasgow demanding £15,000 sterling as 'compensation' for the city not supporting the Jacobite cause. Neither the 'Pretender' nor his troops entered Glasgow, and although the council were afraid of reprisals, they were still canny enough to negotiate. In the end they handed over £5,000 in cash and £500 in goods, and utterly refused to supply the 2,000 broadswords also demanded. Similarly, Paisley was fined £1,000, and paid half of the sum.

By December 1745 Prince Charles Edward was no longer cock o' the walk. His army was in retreat and when he entered Glasgow on Christmas Day (by way of Back Cow Loan, now Ingram Street) his reception was less than enthusiastic. No bells were rung. No local politicians made welcoming speeches. The monies for the local land tax were deliberately not collected by the council, so the Jacobites could not get their hands on the cash. All weapons and ammunition in the city were sent for safe-keeping to the government fortress at Dumbarton. No gentleman even tipped his hat to the prince.

A muster on Glasgow Green netted less than sixty new recruits, mostly criminals and drunkards (one report even says the only man to actually march away with the Jacobites was a debt-ridden shoemaker).

Peeved at the passive resistance, the prince threatened to sack and burn the city. According to tradition he was prevented from so doing by his supporter Cameron of Lochiel. For this reason whenever a Lochiel chief came to Glasgow, he was thereafter to be greeted by the ringing of bells.

The Jacobites' actual revenge came in the usual Glasgow fashion – by plundering the city's wealth. As well as taking free accommodation and food, it was decided to fleece the city's textile manufacturers. A receipt of the time sets out what was supplied:

6,840 yards of woollen cloth for making 4,412 jackets
572 yards of serge
470 yards of plaiding
30 yards of tartan with thread and other trimmings for the
    jackets
25,423 yards of white and check linen for making 12,000 shirts
15lb of thread for sewing the shirts
930 yards of tartan for making 1,240 pair of hose
1,297 pairs of shoes and brogues
3,846 blue bonnets
And 275 yards of packing cloth and two coils of ropes, for baling
    the goods.

RIOT!

If Glasgow wasn't often at the centre of military battles, the opposite was true when it came to civil disorder. Riots have been part of Glasgow street life since 1579, when a pro-Reformation mob attempted to burn down the cathedral, and were successfully resisted (this is the reason why Glasgow has the only complete pre-Reformation cathedral on the Scottish mainland).

Here are some of the city's notable riots:

1606
A local political dispute between the Elphinstones and the Stewarts of Minto brought craftsmen onto the streets armed with bows, swords, pikes and staves. There was extensive damage to property and one man died.

1703
Presbyterian bigots attacked Sir John Bell's house during a service held by the hated Episcopalians. Bell was a former Glasgow magistrate and his erstwhile colleagues swiftly suppressed the tumult.

1725
The Malt Tax Riots, protesting about the imposition of a sixpence tax per barrel of ale. Eight people were shot by troops, and the town house of Daniel Campbell of Shawfield, who had spoken in parliament in favour of the tax, was destroyed – he charged the city several thousand pounds to replace the Glassford Street dwelling.

1780
A major anti-Catholic riot, prompted by the influx of immigrants from the Highlands and Ireland.

1787
Weavers rioted after their wages were slashed. Six were killed by soldiers – the victims being Scotland's first trade union martyrs. The weavers rose again in 1789.

1820
The 'Radical War' fiasco, a supposed working-class insurrection that fizzled out into nothing. Weaver James Wilson, one of the participants, was hanged and beheaded before a crowd of 20,000 on Glasgow Green.

1822
An entirely erroneous belief that a house on Clyde Street was being used for bodysnatching led to a riot of such scale that it had to be quelled by cavalry and infantry with drawn bayonets. It was a miracle that nobody died. Five ringleaders were transported overseas for fourteen years, and one was publicly whipped.

1837
Mass unemployment and widespread poverty led to strikes and violent clashes, with one man being shot dead.

DEUS CUM MACHINA.

1848

Hunger and destitution again saw thousands on the streets, looting and setting up barricades. Seven people were shot by troops. One was a special constable killed by 'friendly fire' – thousands of special constables had been sworn in to help keep the peace.

1909

Rangers and Celtic fans rioted at Hampden Park after the Scottish Cup final ended in a 1–1 draw. Fires were set and property damaged. Many members of the emergency services – police, fire, ambulance – were injured, some seriously.

1919

A riot between white and non-white seamen on Broomielaw led to many shots being fired, causing several injuries.

1919

The Battle of George Square saw tanks, and troops armed with machine guns and field howitzers, facing down 90,000 strikers demanding shorter working hours and better working conditions. The previous day had seen extreme violence between police and protestors, and the raising of the Red Flag. One police officer later died of his injuries. Seen by some authorities as a cataclysmic Bolshevik rising similar to the Russian Revolution of 1917, it caused widespread panic in government circles and cemented the image of 'Red Clydeside'.

1926

Multiple outbreaks of violence accompanied the General Strike, with incidents in Ruby Street, the East End, the city centre, Anderston Cross, Tradeston and Maryhill.

1931

Massive unemployment sparked viciously violent riots in Glasgow Green, Jail Square and Saltmarket.

FIGHTING MEN

Two of the greatest soldiers of the British Empire were both Glasgow lads. Sir Colin Campbell (born 1792) distinguished himself in the thick of battle during the Peninsular War, the Crimea and the Indian Mutiny. Sir John Moore (born 1761) was a hero of the wars against Napoleon, especially in North Africa. He became an icon for British boyhood after his dramatic death in Spain at the Battle of Corunna in 1809.

During the War of 1812 between Britain and the USA, the White House in Washington DC was burned down, the culprits also consuming a meal set out for the congressmen. Although the identity of the exact perpetrators is disputed, the leading candidates are the Royal Scots Fusiliers, a regiment with strong Glasgow connections.

Many ordinary Glaswegians fought in the International Brigade during the Spanish Civil War. In 2010 ninety-seven-year-old Thomas Watters, a former bus driver who volunteered for the frontline Scottish Ambulance Unit, returned to Glasgow to see unveiling of the restored statue of La Pasionaria (The Passion

Flower), a stylised representation of the Republican icon Dolores Ibárruri. The sculpture on Clyde Street bears the inscription:

> The City Of Glasgow and the British Labour Movement pay tribute to the courage of those men and women who went to Spain to fight fascism 1936-1939. 2,100 volunteers went from Britain; 534 were killed, 65 of whom came from Glasgow. Better to die on your feet than live forever on your knees.

LOST BARRACKS

An infantry barracks stood on Gallowgate from 1795.

A cavalry barracks was a feature of Eglinton Street for fifty years from 1821. It was later converted into a poorhouse.

An artillery barracks was set up at Springburn.

Maryhill Barracks, built in 1872, was the city's major military centre for many years. The site is now occupied by housing.

THE FIRST WORLD WAR – THE TROOPS

Many tens of thousands of Glasgow men fought in the First World War. Often they joined up *en masse* by job or affiliation, creating the 'Pals Battalions' such as the Tramways, Boys' Brigade and Chamber of Commerce. Thus the mechanised mass slaughter of trench warfare often annihilated every single young man from a given background, district or occupation.

Of the 3,120 men who joined up from the North British Locomotive Works, 367 were killed. Robert Downie, of the 2nd Battalion Royal Dublin Fusiliers, was awarded the Victoria Cross for his bravery on 23 October 1916.

300 Glasgow policemen enlisted in the early months of the war, depleting the police force so much that further volunteers were discouraged. Constable John McAulay was awarded the Victoria Cross for his actions at the Battle of Cambrai on 27 November 1917. Like many other Glasgow policemen he had joined the Scots Guards. He was one of eight police officers in Britain to win the VC and the only one from Scotland.

Many local men before the war had joined the Glasgow Highlanders Battalion of the Highland Light Infantry; the HLI was a Scottish regiment in the part-time Territorial Force (later the Territorial Army). On 14/15 June 1916 at the Battle of the Somme, the Glasgow Highlanders lost 192 men in just a few minutes. 10,026 men of the HLI were killed during the war. Seven men received Victoria Crosses:

Date	Location	Name
1914	Verneuil	Pte George Wilson
1914	Becelaere	Lt Walter Lorrain Brodie
1915	Givenchy	L/Cpl William Angus (attached to the Royal Scots)
1916	Authuille	Sgt James Youll Turnbull
1917	Ypres	L/Cpl John Brown Hamilton
1918	Bois Favières	Lt-Col William Herbert Anderson
1918	Moeuvres	Cpl David Ferguson Hunter

King George V visited Glasgow in 1917 to present three of the VCs at an outdoor investiture at Ibrox Stadium.

A spectacular memorial to the 7,074 men of the Scottish Rifles regiment who died in the war can be seen outside Kelvingrove

Jock (in captured trench). "Coom awa' up here, Donal'; it's drier."

Museum. It shows three figures – a Lewis gunner firing at the enemy, a dead or wounded young officer, and a sergeant going over the top. The bronze sculpture was unveiled in 1924 by Field Marshal Haig, to a crowd of 10,000.

THE FIRST WORLD WAR – THE HOME FRONT

The well-known writer Neil Munro penned a fiction piece for the *Evening News* in 1908 in which he imagined the German airship fleet attacking Rosyth naval base and the Forth Bridge, and then bombing the Clydeside shipbuilding yards. Fortunately this apocalyptic vision did not materialise during the forthcoming First World War.

Britain's airship production lagged behind the German Zeppelins. The R34 airship, built by the Inchinnan site of William Beardmore's massive complex of armaments manufactories, was launched at the very end of the war, and made its maiden flight in December 1918. The following year it crossed the Atlantic in 75 hours. In 1921 the 643ft-long behemoth was destroyed in an accident.

From 1917 Weirs of Cathcart converted their 'Albert' factory (named after the King of Belgium, whose country was overrun by the conflict) to the manufacture of warplanes. They produced 300 of the B.E.2c (*Blériot Experimental*) two-seater biplane for the Royal Flying Corps, as well as 800 other aircraft, making them the foremost warplane manufacturer on the Clyde. William Douglas Weir (later Baron Weir) became Controller of Aeronautical Supplies at the Ministry of Munitions. As Secretary of State for Air in Lloyd George's Cabinet he united the Royal Flying Corps and the Royal Naval Air Service into the Royal Air Force.

Three more of Weir's factories produced munitions. 'Flanders' was turning out 300,000 6-inch shells a year, while 'Mons' and 'Marne' – both named after trench battles – made hundreds of thousands of 8-inch shells and field gun shells, as well as 100 Medium B tanks and 1,040 Mark VIII tanks. Other tank manufacturers included Beardmore's. By 1918, 90 per cent of Britain's armour plate for tanks was Clyde-built, with 50 tanks a week rolling off the production line.

From the start, the 'Mons' engineering factory was entirely staffed by women (except for the roles of foremen and managers). By June 1916 there were 18,500 women in the metal trades in Glasgow, and half of the city's munitions workers were female. The process of breaking down a complex job usually undertaken by one skilled man, into a series of simpler connected tasks for several allegedly less-skilled women, created tension in the workplace, with unions fighting what they saw as 'dilution' of skills (and hence wages).

Robert Napier's Govan shipyard had been producing warships since 1843, when three gunboats were launched – the first iron-built ships used by the Royal Navy. By the First World War Napier's were building a quarter of all the Navy's new ships.

Other Clydeside shipbuilders were soon contributing to the war effort. Yarrow's yard produced torpedo boat destroyers. D.&W. Henderson churned out 'War Standard' cargo ships. The Fairfield yard near Govan built battleships (HMS *Valiant* and HMS *Howe*), aircraft carriers (HMS *Implacable*) and cruisers (HMS *Norfolk* and HMS *Bellona*), as well as converting its transatlantic liners (such as SS *Campania*) to aircraft carriers. The Clyde-built grand liners of the Anchor Line, SS *Columbia* and SS *Transylvania*, were converted into armed merchant cruisers. And Stephen's of Linthouse built 18 destroyers as well as repairing and refitting an astonishing 9 cruisers, 10 submarines, 38 minesweepers and 120 destroyers.

Also vital to the war were the precision optical instruments made by Barr & Stroud in Anniesland. Their portfolio included rangefinders, gun-sights, bomb-sights, field glasses and periscopes.

False rumours and urban legends spread like wildfire during the war. It was widely believed that vast numbers of Russian troops had secretly landed in Scotland to assist the Allies, and people swore they saw them disembarking at Glasgow, smoking cigars in closed railway carriages, and stamping snow from their boots on station platforms. Foreign waiters and governesses were treated with suspicion, and a widely reported (but fake) 'friend-of-a-friend' story concerned a German servant girl allegedly caught at Bearsden with her trunk full of secret plans and photographs of sensitive sites.

THE SECOND WORLD WAR COMES TO GLASGOW

Glasgow and the Clyde were essential to Britain's survival in the Second World War. On the one hand the area's manufacturing capabilities were immense, producing everything from aircraft and tanks to shells and ships. On the other hand the vast dock frontage, combined with the ability of the Clyde to resist U-boat penetration, meant that Glasgow was Britain's logistical capital during the nation's darkest hour.

In 1940 Britain's gold bullion reserves travelled from London to Glasgow in unmarked railway vans, to be temporarily stored in the Royal Bank of Scotland in Royal Exchange Square while waiting transshipment to Canada. Over £1,800 million in gold and securities were secretly stored in a bank vault in Vancouver.

A mortuary was built beneath the Barrowlands Ballroom in 1940, in anticipation of mass casualties from bombing in the East End. It was never used and the market traders at the Barras stripped out all the valuables and used the space as a stable.

The reality of the conflict was brought home to Glasgow within hours of the declaration of war in September 1939. The SS *Athenia* had recently left Glasgow loaded with people fleeing to North America – as they left, cries of 'Cowards!' were hurled at them from the shipyards. In a breach of the German Navy's own rules of engagement, the liner was torpedoed in the Atlantic, killing 112, including 50 Britons and 30 Americans. The survivors were brought to Greenock and then Glasgow, causing a row about which local council or central government department should pay for what. One of the American passengers, Gustav Anderson, was suspected of photographing military and civil installations for the

Germans, but as he was the citizen of a neutral country he could not be arrested without solid proof. The other American survivors were comforted by the US Ambassador's handsome twenty-two-year-old son – later better known as President John F. Kennedy.

When US forces started arriving in 1942, they were racially segregated. In Glasgow black GIs were invited to social events such as dances and entertainments with no thought of the colour bar, which caused tensions with white American soldiers.

In Evelyn Waugh's novel *Officers and Gentlemen*, his character Trimmer is unable to get a room at the overflowing Central Hotel – an accurate indication of how busy Glasgow was with service personnel.

Glasgow lads Joe Harkin, John McCallum and his brother Jimmy were captured during the retreat from France in 1940. While on a prison work camp in Germany John started a clandestine relationship with a local girl, Traudl. With her help the trio escaped, and made it across occupied Europe to neutral Sweden and eventually Britain. By an astonishing coincidence, they passed unknowingly through the town of Sagan the day after a mass escape by Allied airmen from Stalag Luft Drei – what would later be celebrated as the Great Escape (although, unlike the Glasgow boys, most of the Great Escape airmen were killed or recaptured). The astonishing story was told in John McCallum's book *The Long Way Home: The Other Great Escape*. Traudl, by the way, having waited in vain for several years, eventually married someone else.

THE HOME GUARD

With its headquarters at Park Circus Place, the Glasgow Home Guard had six sub-groups based on the police divisions of Central, Marine, Southern, Northern, Maryhill and Govan. Many works had their own platoon or even a company.

In the early days of the war there was some tension between the police and the air-raid wardens on one hand, and the Home Guard on the other, with the latter sometimes officiously delaying members of the other organisations by insisting on checking identity papers. In the end Chief Constable Percy Sillitoe had to make it quite clear that when it came to Glasgow, it was the police who were in charge.

The Glasgow Area Town Fighting School was set up to train the Home Guard in house-to-house fighting.

150 key points in Glasgow were identified as places for the Home Guard to defend against sabotage. These included wireless stations, shipyards, utilities and factories.

In September 1940 the invasion code word 'Cromwell' was mistakenly issued in Scotland, leading to the ringing of church bells and the hurried mustering of the Home Guard on the look-out for non-existent parachutists.

On 10 May 1941, Rudolf Hess, Hitler's deputy, parachuted down near a farmhouse outside Eaglesham. Giving his name as Hauptmann Albert Horn, he was arrested by the Home Guard, and subsequently transferred to Busby Home Guard Company HQ, then to 3 Battalion Home Guard HQ (or the Scout Hall in Giffnock if you wish), and finally to Maryhill Barracks. During one of these stops he was subjected to an impromptu interrogation by the Home Guard, with translation by a German-speaking clerk from the Polish Consulate – the whole event later attracting the wrath of MI5. Hess spent the rest of his life in confinement. His bizarre peace mission, apparently based on his belief that the Duke of Hamilton would act as a go-between, continues to attract unwarranted conspiracy theories.

For their actions during the Clydebank Blitz, Home Guard Platoon Commander A.R. Ballantyne (2nd Dumbartonshire Battalion) was awarded the George Medal, and Section Leader E. Giblin (4th City of Glasgow Battalion) received the King's Commendation for Brave Conduct.

The Home Guard was stood down in November 1944. The following month 10,000 men from the Glasgow battalions marched past George Square before being formally dismissed.

WE'RE ALL IN IT TOGETHER?

Not surprisingly many accounts of the war emphasise the 'blitz spirit' of everyone pulling together. However, the social and industrial tensions of the 1930s did not go away – and occasionally they boiled over.

In 1941 women workers at the vital Rolls-Royce aero engine complex at Hillington went on strike over pay. More than half the workforce was female, and skilled women were getting 43s a week, while unskilled men were paid 73s. Further industrial action resulted in an improved grading system in 1943, but men were still being paid more than women for decades after.

Also in 1941 an exercise saw the Special Services (later called the Commandos) mount an assault on a Govan factory, in order to test the Home Guard defences. Unfortunately the proceedings were moot, as most of the Home Guard hadn't made it to their posts – because of a bus strike. Strikes were a little-discussed but common fact of life in wartime Glasgow, with stoppages in the shipyards, munitions factories and other vital industries.

VE Day is typically remembered as a time of gaiety and spontaneous street parties. But it did have its darker side in Glasgow. Bonfires in some areas were first fed with timber ransacked from empty homes, the crowds then moving on to strip business premises, and then setting vehicles alight. When the police responded two constables were pushed into a bonfire by a mob in Townhead. There were numerous arrests for hooliganism and assault.

EVACUATION

Fears of intense aerial bombing prompted the authorities to arrange for the evacuation of city schoolchildren, mothers with pre-school offspring, the blind and the disabled. For the majority of people evacuation was voluntary.

Over the 1st, 2nd and 3rd of September 1939, 338 trains were booked to carry 237,523 evacuees from Glasgow. In the event only 118,833 turned up, 50 per cent of the expected total (in Edinburgh the take-up was even less, just 30 per cent). Thirty-five trains were cancelled. In Clydebank again the numbers evacuated were about half those expected. Some people made private arrangements, but many families chose to stay together and risk the bombing.

Unusual evacuation locations included Glen Nevis Youth Hostel at Fort William (the destination for 124 people from Glasgow's Blind Asylum), and Culzean Castle in Ayrshire, which was adapted to host sick children from the Southern General Hospital.

The expected blitzkrieg did not materialise. By January 1940 around three-quarters of the evacuees had drifted back to Glasgow.

As well as the 'pull' of family togetherness, there were also several 'push' factors for the returnees. Glaswegians had been evacuated to Perthshire, Kintyre and Rothesay. Although for some the experience of country or seaside life was positive, even liberating, for others it was disastrous. Catholics were billeted with Protestants and vice-versa. Many slum children had scabies, nits and poor hygiene, not to mention an expectation of urban excitement and facilities. Country people – rich and poor alike – found it difficult to communicate with city kids. Some host families wanted only older boys – so they could work on the farm – or refused to take some kinds of children. Siblings were sometimes split up. Bedwetting was common.

After Clydeside was heavily bombed for the first time in 1941, some 58,000 schoolchildren were evacuated again, joining the 20,000 who had stayed in the country. This time the logistics of the operation were carried out much more smoothly.

Some children were sent to America. One group, having already survived the sinking of their liner *Volendam*, were re-shipped across the Atlantic on the SS *City of Benares* – which was promptly torpedoed, killing seventy-seven children. Forty-six of the survivors spent eight days on a storm-tossed lifeboat, eventually arriving in the Clyde. During the ordeal some of the boys had speculated about getting kilts if they landed in Scotland, so Glasgow Corporation kitted them out appropriately when they were invited to tea with the Lord Provost.

THE BLITZ

Clydeside's strategic importance made it an obvious target for aerial bombardment. However, its distance from most German airfields meant that it got off comparatively lightly compared to industrial centres in England. Even so, Dumbarton, Glasgow, Greenock, Gourock, Paisley and Renfrew were all bombed, and Clydebank suffered one of the most intense attacks of the war.

The first bombs fell on central Glasgow on 19 July 1940, when a lone raider damaged Blawarthill Street in Yoker, killing three people, and Tinto Park football ground in Craigton, injuring thirteen. No alert was sounded. Bombs had fallen on Barrhead on 13 July, followed by an attack on Abbotsinch airfield (they missed), and stray bombs falling on Bridge of Weir, Gleniffer Braes and Hillington.

Dalmarnock and King's Park were targets on 18 September 1940. That night came the first after-dark raid. The subway was knocked out of action at Partick, Henderson's shipyard was damaged, George Square was hit and the cruiser HMS *Sussex*, at anchor in Yorkhill Quay, was set on fire and put out of action for two years (this last titbit remained a secret so the Luftwaffe never knew of their success). Further sporadic raids took place through 1940 and early 1941, with bomb damage in Cathedral Street, John Street, North Frederick Street, Ingram Street, Hospital Street, the High Court, Candleriggs fruitmarket, Tradeston, Garscadden, Hutchesontown, Partick, Hyndland, Kelvinside, Rutherglen, Cathcart, Cambuslang and Burnside.

On 13 March 1941 the first 200-bomber raid of the war targeted Clydebank. Over an eight-hour period 236 bombers dropped 272 tons of high-explosive bombs and 1,650 incendiaries on

Clydebank. Guided by the fires, 203 bombers returned the next night, attacking Clydebank and Glasgow. After the two days 647 people were dead, 16,980 were injured and tens of thousands homeless. The Yarrows and Blythswood shipyards at Scotstoun were badly damaged. The Rolls-Royce aero engine factory was hit, as was the Singer factory, the Royal Ordnance Factory and Yoker Distillery. The fires could be seen for many miles. A part of Maryhill had been flattened. Over 70 per cent of Clydebank was destroyed. Only seven houses in the town remained undamaged.

The fires and the explosions overwhelmed the infrastructure, with water mains damaged, roads blocked, and shelters and first aid centres unable to cope. One Clydebank ambulance crew drove to Glasgow's Western Infirmary and rounded up a group of final year medical students. The superintendent at the hospital refused to give them any supplies because the students were not officially doctors – prompting the ward sister to make sacks out of bedsheets and fill them with bandages and medicines. After assisting at Clydebank the students walked back to Glasgow through the night, two of them to face their exams that day. All of them passed their finals.

The blitz saw many examples of heroism. Among those honoured for their courage during those terrible nights were ambulance driver Hugh Campbell and volunteer ambulance attendant Mary Haldane (both awarded the OBE), district nurse Cecilia McGinty, Dr Daniel Millar and police surgeon Dr John McLaren, all of whom received the MBE, probationer nurse Joan Anderson who got the British Empire Medal, and docker Thomas Denholm, who was awarded the George Medal.

Three police officers, one war reserve constable and five special constables lost their lives during the blitz. Policemen involved in rescuing people from damaged tenements and dealing with the horrors of the bombing were awarded one George Medal, two British Empire Medals, one King's Police Medal, and two Corporation Medals for Gallantry.

Just one enemy aircraft was destroyed during the Glasgow/ Clydebank blitz. The Heinkel 111 was downed by a Blenheim equipped with new radar interception technology. The bomber crashed in Ayrshire.

The last air raid on Glasgow took place in 1943.

AIR DEFENCES

The Anti-Aircraft Control Headquarters of the Royal Artillery was at Aitkenhead House in King's Park. From here orders were issued to gun batteries at Cardross, Kilcreggan, Paisley, Uddingston, Blackhill, Lennoxtown, Garscadden, Clydebank, Old Kilpatrick, Dumbarton and Dykebarhill.

The Observer Corps spotted aircraft from a post on top of the JP Coates factory.

The AA battery at Mid Netherton Farm, Carmunnock, was not supplied with any guns until 5 October 1940. Until that date they hoped to fool the Luftwaffe with some purloined telegraph poles masquerading as gun barrels.

With the threat of invasion receding in 1942, some of the Home Guard were reassigned to anti-aircraft batteries. 1010 Glasgow Home Guard 'Z' Battery became the first Home Guard unit in Scotland to use a new-fangled technology – rockets. The solid-fuel Z rockets were based at Prospecthill Road near Mount Florida, with another battery at Balornock.

The only known case of AA fire bringing down an enemy aircraft over Glasgow took place on 25 March 1943.

In July 1940 there were 120 barrage balloons around the Glasgow/ Renfrew area. Many of the balloons were made in the large indoor space of Kelvin Hall.

The balloons were not always secure, sometimes drifting away. On 1 November 1940 two of them over the Cowal Street Gasworks in Maryhill were struck by lightning and caught on fire.

Air-raid shelters were set up all over the city. George Square had several brick and concrete structures above ground. Trench shelters were dug into Glasgow Green. A railway tunnel near Gallowgate was pressed into use, while another shelter was excavated out of a hillside in Carron Street in Springburn. Some people took cover in the crypt of the Ramshorn Kirk on Ingram Street, while the staff and students of the Glasgow and West of Scotland College of Domestic Science cleaned up a disused sewage tunnel. Many works had their own shelters. During the 1941 blitz eighty workers died at Yarrows when their shelter took a direct hit.

Some of the most bizarre creations of the Second World War were the Starfish decoys. These were patterns of lights or fires created to resemble city streets, factories and airfields – but placed in uninhabited areas to deceive the night-time bombers. These dummy towns were set up at several rural locations, including Craigend near Strathblane, the Lennoxtown and Cumbernauld areas and, south of the Clyde, on Gleniffer Braes near Paisley. The deception diverted many bombs from Clydebank, Dumbarton and Renfrew.

THE 602 (CITY OF GLASGOW) SQUADRON

1925 saw the formation of Glasgow's own air squadron, a light bomber unit based at Renfrew as part of the Auxiliary Air Force (the RAF's equivalent of the Territorial Army). In 1933 602 Squadron moved to a purpose-built airfield at Abbotsinch (now the site of Glasgow Airport). That same year two of their pilots became the first men to fly over and photograph Mount Everest.

In 1939 the 602, now a fighter unit, was incorporated into the RAF and became the first Auxiliary Air Force Squadron to be equipped with the new Spitfires.

In the early months of the Second World War the squadron operated from RAF Drem near Haddington. It is claimed one of their Spitfires fired the first shots in the air war, attacking a German bomber without result in the Firth of Forth on 16 October 1939. Later the same day pilots George Pinkerton and Archie McKellar had the first 'kill' of the air war over Britain, bringing down a Junkers Ju88 off Crail.

The squadron moved to the south of England for the Battle of Britain, where it was in the thick of the action, scoring the second highest toll of enemy aircraft. In total the squadron recorded 150 'kills' during the war.

The history of this incredible unit can be viewed at the 602 (City of Glasgow) Squadron Museum, part of the Royal Highland Fusiliers Museum on Sauchiehall Street. One of the squadron's Spitfires is on display in Kelvingrove Museum.

Among the men associated with 602 were several Free French pilots, and Raymond Baxter, who later went on to fame as a broadcaster with BBC Television, and became particularly associated with the science and technology series *Tomorrow's World*.

THE SECOND WORLD WAR AND THE CLYDE

Without the Clyde receiving and sending off convoys, the Battle of the Atlantic would have been lost – and Britain would have faced starvation and surrender. The Clyde literally saved Britain.

During the war the Clyde shipyards built 1,903 vessels including 304 merchant ships, converted 637 others to war-work, and repaired an astonishing 23,191 ships.

Stephen's of Linthouse refitted or repaired 48 destroyers, 16 aircraft carriers, one battleship and 21 cruisers (including HMS *Sussex*, badly damaged in the Glasgow bombing of July 1940). The passenger liner *Conte Rosso* was still being built at Beardmore's

Dalmuir yard when war was declared. It was requisitioned and swiftly converted in mid-build to the aircraft carrier HMS *Argus*, the world's first carrier with a full-length flight deck.

One of the converted ships was the tramp ship *Empire Penn*, renamed *König Haakon VII* and handed over to the Norwegian government in exile. King Haakon VII had escaped to Britain in 1940. The launch was something of an embarrassment as the new ship collided with another vessel and was damaged. However, the damage was repaired and *König Haakon VII* had a full war service as a merchant vessel and POW repatriation ship.

In 1940 the tanker *San Demetrio*, built in the Blythswood shipyard, was set on fire during a U-boat attack on its Atlantic convoy. The crew abandoned the ship but it remained afloat so at great personal risk they returned the next day, extinguished the flames, and coaxed the stricken vessel to the safe waters of the Clyde. The tanker's precious cargo of aviation fuel was saved.

The much-loved Clyde steamers were sent south and war-converted into tenders, flak ships or minesweepers. Some were used in the evacuation of Dunkirk, where the Victorian paddle-steamer *Waverley* was sunk by a bomb hitting the engine room,

Mercury was lost to a mine, and *Eagle II* ran aground. Other steamers had similar fates – *Marmion* was bombed off Harwich, *Juno* damaged by a landmine in London docks, and *Kylemore* sunk off the east coast in 1941.

Coming in the opposite direction, the English Channel steamer *Maid of Orleans* worked as a tender for the huge troopships docking in the Clyde. *Maid of Orleans* was later converted in a Glasgow shipyard for duties in the European theatre but was sunk by a mine.

Bases on the Clyde were used in the successful attack on the German battleship *Tirpitz*, the Commando raid on the Lofoten Islands, and the evacuation of Spitsbergen.

In Nicholas Monsarrat's novel *The Cruel Sea* (later made into a popular film), the crew of the fictional HMS *Compass* took delivery of their ship in Glasgow.

The Sherbrooke Castle Hotel in Pollokshields was a training school for Merchant Navy radio officers being taught a new and secret technology – radar. The trainees were not allowed to take notes lest they fall into enemy hands.

Glasgow was so important to the Navy it actually had its own Admiral. Vice Admiral Sir J.A.G. Troup was the gaffer of HMS *Spartiate*, a 'stone frigate' better known to its neighbours as the St Enoch Hotel. Under his command were 600 Royal Navy staff spread over 36 buildings throughout the city, all toiling to maintain the enormous logistical effort of the Clyde at war.

The Thames Estuary and the Bristol Channel were full of enemy mines, the east coast ports were vulnerable to E-boats and U-Boats, and the Mersey was frequently bombed. The Clyde was therefore Britain's safest troop harbour.

The unique scale of the King George V Dock allowed large vessels such as troopships, aircraft carriers, convoy escort vessels and armed merchantmen to 'parallel park' along either side of dock.

Between May 1942 and December 1944, 339 troopships arrived on the Clyde, bringing with them a total of 1,319,089 American soldiers, all of whom needed to be disembarked and, often, put straight onto massive troop trains.

The build up to Operation Torch, the invasion of Algiers in 1942, saw almost 300 troopships and naval vessels assemble in the Firth of Clyde. A similar fleet gathered for the invasion of Sicily in 1943. Without the King George V Dock, the other quays and harbours, and the Clyde's unmatched defences against U-boats, these crucial episodes in the Allied assault on the Axis powers would not have been possible.

During preparations for D-Day the Mulberry Harbours were assembled in Lanarkshire and towed by ships from Glasgow. During the actual landings the harbours were directed from their HQ ship HMS *Aristocrat* (formerly the Rothesay steamer *Talisman*).

Perhaps the strangest story of the war at sea was recounted in Peter Haining's book *The Jail That Went To Sea*. In 1941 the demand for merchant seamen was greater than the supply, so unconventional tactics were employed. Three members of the Protestant street gang the Billy Boys, plus two stalwarts of their hated Catholic rivals, the Norman Conks, were all released from Barlinnie prison on the same day – and gently persuaded to sign up for a transatlantic trip. Once at sea the five buried their differences and got on with shirking any hard work, getting drunk at every opportunity, and nearly fomenting mutiny. Wherever they got shore leave – Montreal, Philadelphia and Halifax – miniature crime waves coincidentally took place. William McCormack (the Billy Boys) and Bobbie McCourt (the Conks) formed a partnership and went AWOL in New York, where it is thought they blended into the city's violent underworld. The other three were discharged on US soil some time later, and were never heard from again. It wasn't quite *The Dirty Dozen*.

WAR WORK

Glasgow was the workshop of the war, turning out immense numbers of munitions and war-related products.

Rolls-Royce's main works was based at Crewe, within easy reach of the German bombers, so a 'shadow factory' was constructed at Hillington. This became the largest aero engine factory in the world, six times larger than its parent plant. Here between 1940 and 1945, 10,000 workers manufactured or repaired 50,000 Merlin engines, the technology at the heart not only of the Spitfire but also the Hurricane, Kittyhawk, Beaufighter, Mustang and Mosquito fighters, and the Halifax, Whitley, Wellington and Lancaster heavy bombers. The Merlin could be said to be the engine that helped win the war.

The Springburn railway works turned out 1.6 million bombs and shells, 13,000 mines, large numbers of tanks and war locomotives – and 800 dough-mixing bowls destined for the galleys of the Royal Navy.

When King George VI and Queen Elizabeth (later the Queen Mother) visited the North British Locomotive Works in 1942, the queen asked one of the apprentices what he was making.
 'Time-and-a-hauf, mum!' he quickly replied.

H. Morris & Co., who had been furniture manufacturers before the war, converted their operation to the production of everything from rifles and ammunition boxes to landing barge pontoons, aircraft jettison tanks, stabilisers for barrage balloons, and helicopter blades. One of their projects – a flying jeep with twin-bladed rotors – never got off the ground. Blackie & Son, the printing company at Bishopbriggs, found themselves making shells, while J. & G. Weir at Cathcart turned out field gun carriages and anti-tank guns.

One of the most diverse of war suppliers was the Scottish Co-operative Workers' Society. The Co-op had been at the heart of many a Glasgow working-class life, and now it was at the heart of war production. Its sheet metal works at Shieldhall manufactured

230,000 'Flying Dustbin' heavy mortar shells, 55,000 bunks for Anderson shelters, over 10,000 bomb cases and 8,000 cordite cases – not to mention 150-gallon drop-tanks for Thunderbolt fighters. Many of the ovoid drop-tanks saw post-war service as children's boats in Glasgow's parks. The SCWS motor body and cartwright department in Scotland Street produced 750 tank transporters, while the SCWS boot and shoe factory made 607,500 pairs of service boots, the hosiery factory turned out 1,835,270 military essentials including underwear, socks, woollens, uniforms and flying suits, and the sundries department filled 742,248 tins with powdered egg and 1,137,672 containers with milk powder. And the SWCS paper and print depot at Eastfield, Cambuslang, supplied official forms and paper goods, including the forms for letters home distributed to German POWs.

4

CRIME &
PUNISHMENT

THE MAJESTY OF THE LAW

A magistrate in eighteenth-century Gorbals imposed a fine of half a guinea on a man accused of a serious assault. When informed by a court official that the case had yet to be tried, never mind a conviction achieved, the bailie thought for a moment. 'In that case,' he pronounced, 'we'll just make the fine five shillings.'

In the early days of court-based trials the jury were rewarded with half a guinea apiece if they found for the prosecution. During a Glasgow trial the counsel for the Crown reminded the jury of this bonus, at which point the accused – a wealthy merchant – shouted from the dock that he would double the fee if they found him not guilty. The judge rebuked him for attempting to bribe the jury.

In 1593 George Smollett, a burgess (an accredited merchant) of Dumbarton, used a dodgy royal warrant to illegally impound goods and animals coming from the Highlands and Islands to markets in Glasgow and Renfrew. Not content with theft, he also had the Highland traders imprisoned so that they could not reclaim their property. As a result it was reported that the Highlanders had conceived 'a deadly hatred of the burghs of Glasgow and Renfrew' and were planning reprisals. Glaswegian highhegians went to have a word with Smollett, but he skipped town.

Flamboyant defence lawyer Joseph Beltrami is a veteran of over 500 murder trials. He gained the first ever Royal Pardon issued in Scotland when he had Maurice Swanson's conviction for bank robbery overturned. He famously campaigned for the release of Patrick Meehan, who had been convicted of a murder in 1969. When Meehan's sentence was finally quashed, lawyer and client spoiled the success by having a very public falling-out.

'POUR ENCOURAGER LES AUTRES'

When the Marquis of Montrose was executed in Edinburgh in 1650, his body was dismembered and distributed round the country. One of his legs was nailed up in Glasgow, to remind people of the fate reserved for traitors.

When Montrose was outlawed by proclamation at Glasgow Cross, a man named John Bryson spontaneously shouted out that the Marquis was 'as honest a nobleman as was in this kingdom.' The Glasgow magistrates promptly arrested Bryson and had him incarcerated in a filthy prison.

The so-called rebels of the 1666 Pentland Rising in the Lothians were treated appallingly on capture. Four of their severed heads were placed on spikes on Glasgow's Tolbooth. Their sympathisers climbed the tower under cover of darkness and removed the grisly exhibits.

In 1694 a fervent Glaswegian Jacobite was convicted of sedition through persuading soldiers to desert. He was placed in the pillory with a paper on his head reading: 'John McLachlan, schoolmaster at Glasgow, appointed to be set on the pillory at Edinburgh and Glasgow, and sent to the plantations, for seducing and debauching soldiers to run away from their colours, and desert their majesties' service.'

In 1723 George Cowan, a Glasgow merchant, was forced to stand in the pillory bearing a sign reading 'George Cowan, A Notorious Fraudulent Bankrupt'.

Weaver and former policeman Richard Campbell, the ringleader of a riot in 1822, was dragged behind a cart along Trongate and Gallowgate and given 20 lashes at every major crossroads – 80 lashes in all. He then had salt rubbed into his wounds. This was the last public flogging in Glasgow.

In 1587 the Glasgow kirk session had a lever built on the Broomielaw, so that malevolent gossips and other female miscreants could be ducked in the Clyde, while the kirk elders looked on from on high at Glasgow Bridge.

In 1643 the Glasgow kirk session declared that unrepentant fornicators should be chained for three hours in the jougs, then publicly whipped and imprisoned or banished from the town.

In 1574 married couple Alexander Curry and Marion Smith were warned off fighting with each other. If either struck the other they would be 'brankit', that is, they would be displayed in public with their mouth stopped up by the distressingly uncomfortable iron bridle known as the branks.

In 1928 a part-time soldier in the Territorial Army spotted a crow from a moving train near Glasgow, and fired at it with his rifle. The bullet landed 2 miles away, killing a young woman walking with her fiancé on Cathkin Braes. The soldier received a three-month sentence for recklessly discharging his weapon.

THE EXPERIENCE OF WOMEN

In 1697 Captain Douglas of Sir William Douglas's regiment, along with a fellow officer and a corporal, was found guilty of raping a servant girl in Glasgow. The normal penalty would have been execution, but Captain Douglas, being a gentleman in the king's service, was let off with a fine of 300 merks.

Jean Key, a young widow and heiress from Balfron, was abducted, raped and forcibly married to Robin Oig, Rob Roy's son. When a legal challenge prevented the MacGregors from obtaining her money, she escaped her captors' clutches and ended her days in Glasgow, dying at an early age in 1751.

MURDER MOST FOUL

In 1694 Major James Menzies, commanding officer of Lord Lindsay's regiment, then quartered in Glasgow, got into a row with the local magistrates in the council chamber and ran his

MURDER MADE EASY.

"ACONITE, SIR? WE ONLY SELL POISONS TO MEDICAL MEN; BUT ANYTHING IN REVOLVERS AND DYNAMITE"——!!!

sword through Robert Park, the Town Clerk. Menzies ordered his soldiers to blockade the street and escaped on horseback to Gorbals. He was shot during a fight with a posse. The army raised a charge of murder against his pursuers – the case was found not proven.

Much-loved Glasgow author Jack House introduced a new phrase into the local psychogeography with his celebrated 1961 book *Square Mile of Murder*. The area described in the book covered west central Glasgow, and featured four of the most notorious murder cases of Victorian and Edwardian times:

1. Dr Edward William Pritchard was hanged for poisoning three people, including his wife, in Sauchiehall Street and Berkeley Street.

2. Madeleine Smith of Blythswood Square, declared not proven for the murder of her lover Pierre Emile L'Angelier, attracted huge notoriety because of the explicitness of the pair's love letters.

3. Jessie McLachlan was found guilty of murdering her friend Jessie McPherson in Sandyford Place at Charing Cross, but almost certainly was not the killer. Her sentence of hanging was commuted.

4. Oscar Slater was imprisoned in 1908 for a murder on West Princes Street – a crime he did not commit. Slater remained in prison until 1928. Detective Lieutenant Trench, who exposed the nature of the miscarriage of justice against Slater, was dismissed from the force and had his reputation sullied.

HANGED BY THE NECK UNTIL YE BE DEAD

'You'll die facing the Monument' was a common insult thrown at badly behaved miscreants, meaning they were destined to be hanged in Jail Square (now Jocelyn Square), facing Nelson's Monument on Glasgow Green.

Between 1814 and 1865, seventy-two people were executed 'facing the Monument'. Of these, five were women, all condemned for murder. The most common crimes committed by the men were murder, robbery, housebreaking and forgery.

Other, less familiar capital crimes – unique to Scottish law – included *hamesucken* (entering into a house to commit violence) and *strouthrief* (theft with violence in a person's house). Peter Gray was hanged for the former in 1798.

Before Jail Square became the standard place for public execution in 1814, there had been various gallows sites: at Gallowmure, on the north side of Gallowgate (which is how the thoroughfare got its name); at Howgate Head north of the cathedral (now under the M8); on the site of the former Bishop's Castle next to the cathedral (now the Royal Infirmary); and finally at Glasgow Cross.

After 1865 the executions took place out of the public gaze, within the walls of Duke Street prison. From 1946 all hangings took place at Barlinnie prison.

James Wilson, found guilty of high treason in 1820, was given special treatment – he was hanged and then beheaded with an axe.

In the eighteenth century condemned men with backgrounds of religious or political opposition often made speeches from the scaffold. To drown out such seditious addresses, the Glasgow magistrates ordered the military guard to loudly beat their marching drums.

In 1797 the notorious James McKean was hanged for murder. Patches of his skin were removed, tanned, and sold as leather mementos.

Glasgow hangmen frequently supplemented their meagre fees by selling souvenirs from the condemned, such as hair or clothes, as well as cut-up sections of the noose.

Glasgow's last public execution was in 1865, when 30,000 turned out to see the end of Dr Edward William Pritchard, who had poisoned three members of his family. Rumours later abounded that building works uncovered Pritchard's boots in a secret underground niche. It was speculated that the hangman had intended to sell them as souvenirs, but had been dismissed before he could return for them.

In 1798 the executioner was too nervous to do his job, so the Lord Provost, John Dunlop, pushed him aside and pulled the bolt that launched murderer John McMillan into eternity.

In 1770 murderer Andrew Marshall tried to escape his fate by leaping up to grasp the gallows arm just as the noose was placed around his neck. The executioner eventually got him down by beating him with a stick. After the execution Marshall's body was tarred and hung in chains.

In 1851 the seventy-four-year-old semi-invalid hangman John Murdoch bungled the execution of Archibald Hare, so that the prisoner writhed in agony at the end of a too-short drop.

In 1890 the hanging of murderer Henry Devlin at Duke Street prison went badly wrong and he died of strangulation – very slowly.

PRISONS

The principal prison from the 1620s onward was the combined tolbooth, courthouse and jail, at the corner of High Street and Trongate. Although most of the building was demolished in 1921, the tall steeple still remains. Severed heads were once upon a time fixed to its spikes.

Prisons were often places where the rich and powerful could keep inconvenient people out of the way, without bothering with all the inconveniences of pesky things like trials. In 1666 William Drew petitioned to be set free from the Tolbooth, on the grounds that he had been incarcerated without trial for five years by the Laird of Keir.

A year later one of Glasgow's frequent fires threatened the Tolbooth. The magistrates refused to evacuate those inside, so the townspeople assembled ladders and freed the prisoners.

Eight prisons were operating in Glasgow in the early nineteenth century, but most closed and eventually the only ones left were the Burgh Jail at Glasgow Green and the Bridewell on Duke Street. The latter 'House of Correction' first opened for business in 1798 and following major developments became Glasgow's main prison for over a century.

Under the direction of William Brebner (1783–1845) Duke Street was regarded as a model institution, providing work and healthy living for the inmates.

Charles Dickens visited Duke Street in 1847 and called it 'a truly damnable jail'.

In 1843 the prison chaplain stated, 'Of the many thousands annually imprisoned, I think it would not be possible to find 100 sober criminals in any one year.'

The same chaplain described how an alcoholic weaver, 'W.B.', voluntarily entered Duke Street – even though he had committed no crime – in the hope that the regime would cure his addiction. According to the report, the drastic intervention worked.

There are several variations of the popular street song about Duke Street, 'There is a Happy Land'. Here is one version:

> There is a happy land, down in Duke Street Jail.
> Where all the prisoners lie, tied to a nail.
> Bread and water for their tea, ham and eggs they never see.
> There they live in miser-ee . . .
> God save the Queen!

Barlinnie prison opened in the East End in 1882 although Duke Street continued in operation until the 1950s.

Hangings took place inside the walls of both prisons. The first men to be hanged at Duke Street were murderers Henry Mullen and Martin Scott, in 1883. The last double execution also took place at Duke Street, when James Rollins and Albert Fraser were despatched in 1920.

Susan Newell, one of the few female murderers to be hanged in the twentieth century, breathed her last at Duke Street in 1923. The hangman, John Ellis, disliked hanging women and, possibly affected by the nature of his job, eventually committed suicide.

The last hanging in Glasgow was in 1960, when Anthony Miller walked to the scaffold at Barlinnie. His was the penultimate execution in Scotland.

The 'Bar-L', as Barlinnie is nicknamed, is one of the most notorious prisons in Britain. From 1973 it was home to the Special Unit, a radical attempt at reforming some of the most violent men in the prison system. Notable successes included murderers Hugh Collins and Jimmy Boyle, who when released went on to have successful careers as writers and sculptors. But the Special Unit seemed to lose its way and it closed in the mid-1990s after great controversy.

GANGS

Violent street gangs have been a feature of Glasgow criminal life since at least the 1880s, when a Townhead group called the Penny Mob started to garner press attention.

Most gangs were geographically related, operating on a 'turf' which could be as big as a district or limited to just one street. Many were formed along sectarian lines.

In the early days some journalists were so taken by the colourful names the gangs gave themselves – the Hi Hi, the Ping Pong, the San Toy, the Village Boys, the Redskins, the Norman Conks, the Tongs – that they overlooked the sheer horror of the violence involved. In March 1924, during a fight between the Bridgegate Boys and the Parlour Boys at the Bedford Parlour Dance Hall in Celtic Street, James 'Razzle-Dazzle' Dalziel was fatally stabbed.

The generic name for Glasgow hooligans used to be 'keelies'. These days the universal term is 'neds'.

ROB DA BANK

In 1811 the Glasgow office of the Paisley Union Bank on Ingram Street was relieved of tens of thousands of pounds. Pursued to London, one of the robbers was arrested and, astonishingly, negotiated a free pardon for himself in exchange for handing over part of the cash (this gentleman was later hanged for robbing a mail coach). Another of the gang returned to Edinburgh where his Paisley Union notes were impounded by a bank whose suspicions were aroused. A gallus chap, he promptly sued the bank – but he lost the case, and found himself arrested for the robbery. He committed suicide three days before he was due to be hanged. Most of the rest of the money was recovered twelve years later.

A flood of forged Union Bank of Scotland notes in 1866 led police to suspect that photographer John Henry Greatrex of Sauchiehall Street had been counterfeiting banknotes using a lithographic

printing process. Greatrex moved on to Aberdeen and then fled to America, the police one step behind. In New York the Glasgow cops cunningly bagged Greatrex's female accomplice by placing an advertisement for a photographic assistant, stating 'a Scotch girl preferred'. Greatrex was jailed while the detective who had pursued him, Superintendent McCall, went on to become Chief Constable of Glasgow.

In 1971 an armed duo raided the Clydesdale Bank at St George's Cross. The robbers' getaway vehicle of choice was a tad unusual – they took the subway. Not surprisingly they were caught, and went to jail for ten years.

THE POLIS – THE EARLY DAYS

In 2008 the Advertising Standards Authority forced the Metropolitan Police to stop claiming that they were the oldest police force in the world. Although the Bow Street Runners preceded Glasgow's finest, the Met itself was not formally created until 1829 – and the City of Glasgow Police were formed in 1800. So Glasgow is officially home to the world's oldest police force.

Two earlier attempts to set up a professional police force, in 1779 and 1788, both faltered through lack of finance and political will. In each case the force consisted of just eight men, but the principles of 'preventive policing' were being practiced in Glasgow forty years before they were enshrined by Sir Robert Peel in London.

The first Master of Police was John Stenhouse, a Glasgow merchant. The force totalled nine men on patrol (three on any one shift), plus sixty-eight watchmen who watched fixed points during the night.

The early police multi-tasked, calling the hours ('It's five o'clock and a rainy morning'), dealing with fires and even sweeping the streets. The latter task netted horse dung worth £450 in one year, a useful supplement to the force's fledgling finances.

Despite doing what we think of as non-police work, the first Glasgow cops were undoubtedly effective, causing criminals to move out of the city to south of the river. In response a police force was established in Gorbals in 1808.

In the early years each police force operated solely in its own administrative area, such as a burgh. Many burghs did not have police (largely because the local politicians did not want to pay for them). Forces were created in Calton in 1819 and Anderston five years later. In 1846 Glasgow Police swallowed up both of them, along with Gorbals, giving a combined strength of 360 police officers. A decade on, the independent Maryhill Burgh Police was formed, followed two years later by Partick Burgh Police and the Clyde Police, who patrolled the docks. Govan Burgh started its force in 1864.

Barrhead was a popular place for a drunken punch-up on Saturday night, as for much of the nineteenth century it had neither jail nor police force.

Policemen in the early Victorian period weren't always the pick of the bunch. In the first half of 1847, for example, 11 went absent without leave, 20 were let go because they were 'worn out', 4 were kicked out for assaulting prisoners, 48 simply resigned and 71 officers were dismissed for being drunk on duty. The total of 154

Absent-minded Detective. "SPEAK UP PLEASE!"

represented around a third of the total workforce – but there were 173 new recruits to replace them.

Policemen wore tall or top hats until the early 1870s when helmets were introduced. Most Strathclyde Police officers now wear caps.

Officers sometimes wore leather neckbands to protect them from being slashed with a razor from behind.

In the 1860s the dreadful overcrowding in poor areas prompted the council to measure tenements and give them 'tickets' displaying the size of the dwelling and the number of people permitted to live there. Bizarrely, this duty fell on the police. Several officers consequently died of typhus.

Glasgow's first professional detective was appointed in 1819, when Lieutenant Peter McKinlay was promoted to the new post of Criminal Officer. McKinlay was the forerunner of all the CID detectives in Britain's police forces.

The Glasgow Detective Department was formally created in 1821, twenty-three years before Sir Robert Peel formed a detective squad at Scotland Yard in London.

Lieutenant was a rank peculiar to Scottish forces, along with Intendant, a title meaning supervisor or senior officer. Neither title is now used, although the latter partly survives in the rank of Superintendant.

For decades the Procurator Fiscal did not feel the detectives had sufficient experience or skills to deal with murder cases, so Glasgow CID did not investigate its first murder until 1862. This turned out to be the Sandyford Murder – and they nabbed the wrong person (Jessie McLachlan), letting the real killer go free.

So perceptive were the skills of Detective Lieutenant Archie Carmichael (CID 1869–1900) that he was known as 'Glasgow's Sherlock Holmes'.

Technological innovations included the use of the electric telegraph for communications in 1861, photography of criminals in 1862, a horse-drawn prisoners' van (1878), telephones (1880–6), a river patrol boat in 1881 (actually a rowing boat) and fingerprint

records (1899). Perhaps the most utilised police tool was the two-wheeled 'drunk barrow' used to transport over 100 intoxicated citizens to the cells each weekend.

In the 1890s the Glasgow police were widely regarded as the most physically imposing body of men in the country. Their tug-of-war team retained the world title year after year (its captain was William McIntosh, the father of the famous artist Charles Rennie Mackintosh). The team's anchor, Constable Alexander Kennedy, stood 6ft 2in in his stockinged feet and weighed 28 stone. It was often claimed that Kennedy, a champion hammer-thrower, shot-putter and caber-tosser, was the world's biggest policeman.

Perhaps the least glorious moment in the force's history came in 1882 when they were required to send over thirty men to Skye to assist in the eviction of crofters who had dared to resist their avaricious landlords. The sight of burly officers removing penniless women and children from their hovels during 'The Battle of the Brae' was widely and negatively reported.

By the time the City of Glasgow Police was celebrating its centenary, it had a staff of 1,355, which was 1,246 more than a hundred years earlier. Over 58,000 arrests were made annually, of which more than 22,000 (or 38 per cent) were for assault and disorderly conduct, mostly related to drunkenness.

THE POLIS IN THE TWENTIETH CENTURY

The police bought their first motor vehicle – a prison van – in 1911. The first two police cars did not arrive until 1921, with one being reserved for the chief constable and the other used by CID. For many years most detectives still travelled to crime scenes by public transport.

In 1936 a network of patrol cars with two-way radio was established. Personal radios had to wait for another thirty years.

With the force depleted by officers volunteering for the army in the First World War, new recruitment initiatives included the appointment in 1915 of Glasgow's first policewoman, Miss Emily Miller. Ten further female officers arrived four years later. The Second World War saw 220 recruits for the Women's Auxiliary Police Corps.

Of the 748 Glasgow policemen who had enlisted to fight in the First World War, 173 were confirmed killed or missing presumed dead – a casualty rate of over 23 per cent. 339 police officers enlisted during the Second World War; 30 of them were killed – a casualty rate of 9 per cent. Officers serving in the armed forces won the OBE, the British Empire Medal, the Military Medal and bar, the Distinguished Conduct Medal, the Distinguished Flying Medal and three Distinguished Flying Crosses.

In 1932 Chief Constable Percy Sillitoe introduced black and white chequered cap bands. 'Diced' designs based on the original 'Sillitoe Tartan' are now found on police uniforms all over the world. Sir Percy brought his gangbusting techniques from Sheffield to tackle Glasgow's street gangs, and later in his career he became the Director-General of MI5.

The Second World War saw the police expanding their role into security. One notable success was the arrest of Alphonse Timmerman, a Belgian merchant seaman posing as a refugee who landed at Clydebank on 1 September 1941. Hidden writing materials showed he was a German spy. He was executed at Wandsworth prison in July 1942.

In 1950 Constable James Robertson was executed for the murder of his girlfriend. In 1969 Howard Wilson, a former constable turned career criminal, killed two officers and seriously injured a third. He received life imprisonment.

15 May 1975 saw the creation of Strathclyde Police, a regional force including not just Glasgow but also constabularies from Ayrshire, Argyll, Dunbartonshire, Lanarkshire and Renfrew & Bute. Strathclyde is the largest of the eight Scottish police forces, with headquarters on Pitt Street in the centre of Glasgow.

THE POLIS TODAY

In 2006/7 Strathclyde Police recorded 426,018 crimes and offences across its entire area, which includes much of western Scotland. 77 of these were murders or cases of culpable homicide (the Scottish legal term for manslaughter). In the same year there were 19,502 road crashes, of which 88 involved at least one death.

The current staffing level, including civilian posts, is over 10,000.

The Strathclyde Police Pipe Band, under its Pipe Major Ian McLellan BEM, won the World Pipe Band Championship for the first time in 1976, and clocked up another eleven world titles, including six successive years in a row from 1981.

The force has Scotland's only police helicopter.

TERRORISM

In 1883 bombs exploded simultaneously at three locations around Glasgow. Tradeston Gas Works in Lilybank Street (now Gourock Street) was set on fire, the flames spreading to adjacent factories and injuring eleven people. Slight damage was caused to Buchanan Street railway station, and an explosion on the aqueduct at Possil Road failed to breach the Forth & Clyde Canal – had it done so the flood damage would have been immense. The culprits were the Ribbon Society, an offshoot of the Irish Republican organisation the Fenian Brotherhood. Five men were found guilty and received penal servitude for life.

In 1921 around thirty armed men attacked the prisoner delivery van as it conveyed senior IRA officer Francis (Frank) Carty from an appearance at the Central Police Court to Duke Street prison. Inspector Robert Johnston was killed and Detective Sergeant George Stirton badly wounded, but the IRA gang failed to open the van doors and the mission was abandoned without achieving its goal. The bullet holes from 'The Battle Of Rottenrow' can still be seen on a wall in Duke Street. Police attempts to arrest suspects created a full-scale riot in the Irish areas of the East End. Despite this a search of an address in Abercrombie Street turned up Scotland's largest-ever arms cache – gelignite, grenades, dozens of rifles and handguns, ammunition, and a home-made bomb. No-one was ever successfully tried for the murder of the police officer.

In 2007 terrorists attempted to drive a carbomb into the main terminal of Glasgow Airport. The Queen's Commendation for Bravery was awarded to seven men who helped foil the attack – Sergeant Torquil Campbell and PC Stewart Ferguson, both of Strathclyde Police, and civilians Stephen Clarkson, Michael Kerr, Harry Lambie, Michael McDonald and Alex McIlveen. Baggage handler John Smeaton, who was at the heart of the action, was awarded the Queen's Gallantry Medal.

A POLICEMAN'S LOT

Between 1909 and 1948 twenty-five other officers were awarded the King's Police Medal for Gallantry.

The Carnegie Hero Fund Trust posthumously honoured PC David Peterson (1972) and PC Colin MacDuff (1973) for selfless acts of bravery.

Several officers during Victorian times were commended for their bravery in halting runaway horses, a particularly common and dangerous urban hazard. In 1895 PC Robert Murray was fatally injured trying to stop a runaway horse and coal lorry.

'IT'S A TARDIS!' – GLASGOW'S POLICE BOXES

The first police boxes in Britain appeared in Glasgow in 1891. The fourteen slim cast-iron hexagons were painted red and equipped with a telephone. They were crowned with prominent gas-powered lights for summoning the beat officers, the system controlled from the central police station.

In the 1930s a new generation of police boxes flourished, 323 being in place by 1938, giving the highest ratio of boxes to police officers in the country. These were 'Mark I' boxes, timber-structured rectangles that are now universally familiar because Doctor Who's TARDIS was based on the design.

Unlike the London police boxes (and the TARDIS), Glasgow's examples were all painted red until the late 1960s. After this time some were repainted in blue. Each box contained a telephone, incident book, fire extinguisher and first-aid kit, and served as police station in miniature for bobbies on the beat.

Four police boxes remain on the streets of Glasgow, and are the last original 1930s boxes still on the streets of Britain. They can be seen at: Cathedral Square, the Wilson Street/Glassford Street intersection, the corner of Buchanan Street and Gordon Street, and where Great Western Road meets Byres Road. The latter two have been converted to bijou coffee dispensaries, with the West End outlet going by the name of 'Coppuchino'. All four boxes are category B-listed historic monuments.

There is also a red police box in the Museum of Transport, and a blue one in the Summerlee Museum of Scottish Industrial Life at Coatbridge.

5

TRANSPORTS OF DELIGHT

ROAD TRANSPORT BEFORE THE MOTOR CAR

The first stagecoach service between Glasgow and Edinburgh started in 1678, but it failed because the roads were so bad. Most gentlemen preferred to travel on horseback because it was faster and more reliable.

In 1688 the roads between the two cities were in such a state that, when noblemen travelled in a coach drawn by six horses, they had to have footmen running alongside each side of the vehicle to keep it upright.

The 'Edinburgh and Glasgow Caravan' ran in 1749, taking a full two days to cover the 44 miles. Nine years later, a stagecoach called 'The Fly' was doing the business in just twelve hours, including a stop for a meal. It was not until 1799 that the journey was cut to six hours. Competition saw the time reduced to four and a half hours, but when the Edinburgh and Glasgow Railway opened in 1842 the stagecoaches ceased.

The stagecoach service between Glasgow and London only started in 1788. The 405 miles were covered in 65 hours, or the best part of three days. Rival Glasgow stagecoaches, owned or hired by inn proprietors, departed from the Buck's Head and the Saracen's Head, each service enticing passengers with claims of improved comfort or convenience. In 1789 a one-way ticket was 9s 6d.

Until 1777 just two men were employed to clean, maintain and repair all of Glasgow's roads. The state of the streets can be imagined.

A steam-driven stagecoach service briefly operated between Glasgow and Paisley in the 1830s. The Steam Carriage Company of Scotland was based in George Square. In about 1834 the boiler exploded on the road to Paisley, killing several people. This, combined with opposition and dirty tricks from other transport operators, caused the enterprise to fold.

The Glasgow to Carlisle road was built by the engineer Thomas Telford. Its construction and viaducts became the model for future civil engineers.

THE ROADS TODAY

The Glasgow area is criss-crossed by motorways – the endlessly busy M8, plus the M73 and M74 heading south, the M80 north, and the M77 to Ayrshire and Prestwick Airport.

In 2001 just over half the households in Glasgow had no car. This was put down to the difficulty of parking in many areas, plus the widespread availability of buses, suburban trains and the subway. In the larger Glasgow 'travel to work' area, however, more than three-quarters of all journeys are made by car. Bicycle use is very low, although the cycle network is expanding, with over 140 miles of designated cycle-friendly routes in existence.

There are around 40 bus companies in Greater Glasgow, the dominant player being First Bus, who account for 70 per cent of all bus-miles.

CANALS

Daniel Defoe, in his *Tour of Scotland* (1726), recommended that, as the Firth of Clyde and the Firth of Forth were only 14 miles apart, they should be joined by a canal, known then as a 'navigation'. The word gave rise to the name 'navvies' for the men who laboured to build the canals (and later the railways).

The Forth & Clyde Canal took twenty-two years and £300,000 to build, opening in 1790. It left the Clyde at Bowling, east of Dumbarton, and ran north-east towards Falkirk, with a branch to Port Dundas in central Glasgow.

The construction of the canal created the burgh of Maryhill, named after Mary Hill, the wife of Robert Graham, the owner of the former country estate through which the canal passed.

Although part of the canal in the city centre has been built over, it is still extant through Clydebank, Drumchapel, Kelvindale, Possil, Bishopbriggs, Kirkintilloch, Kilsyth and beyond. A stretch, complete with several locks, is a popular visit in Maryhill.

In 1802 the stern-wheel steamer *Charlotte Dundas* towed two loaded sloops, each carrying 70 tons, from Lock 20 on the canal to Port Dundas, the 19 miles covered in six hours against a strong wind. This was the world's first commercial application of a steamship.

The Monkland Canal, completed in the 1790s and designed by James Watt, ran east from Port Dundas. Parts still exist in the Coatbridge area.

1840 saw the opening of Glasgow's shortest canal, the ½ mile-long Forth & Cart Canal, linking the Forth & Clyde Canal to the River Clyde. The entrance at Whitecrook near Clydebank was directly opposite the mouth of the River Cart, the idea being to link Paisley with the grand trans-Scotland canal.

Canals boosted Glasgow's industrial expansion but were swiftly eclipsed by the railways. In the early nineteenth century the Glasgow & Paisley Canal was carrying 1,000 passengers daily. These days it has all but entirely disappeared, just leaving names such as Paisley Canal train station.

GLASGOW'S EARLY RAILWAYS

Glasgow's first railway – in the sense of something that ran along rails – was built in 1826, a 10-mile track from the Monklands coalfield downhill to the Forth & Clyde Canal at Kirkintilloch. On the way down gravity did the work, while horses pulled the trucks back up the slope. The coal then proceeded by barge to Glasgow.

1831 saw the opening of the first steam-powered railway, the Garnkirk & Glasgow, which brought coal from Monklands through Gartloch, Cradowan, Garnkirk and Hogganfield. Its terminus was in Townhead, next to the Tennent works, which used 30,000 tons of coal a year.

George Stephenson of *Rocket* fame was commissioned to build two locomotives for the opening, *St Rollox*, weighing 4 tons and costing £750, and the 8-ton *George Stephenson*. On 7 July 1831 twenty-four specially invited VIPs travelled on a private trip in the carriage *Isabella*, the first railway passenger vehicle made in Glasgow. The engine briefly reached a maximum speed of 22mph.

On the second trial ten days later the locomotive hit a rock and overturned, injuring three people, one seriously. The obstruction had been placed by someone in the road transport industry, one of the 'dirty tricks' typical of the cut-throat competition between rival industries.

The official opening on 27 September 1831 was the first public service to run in Scotland and only the second in Britain. Two trains ran, one filled with thrill-seeking passengers and the other carrying thirty-three wagons loaded with coal, iron, freestone, lime and grain. Hundreds of people gathered at Provan Mill, where the two trains passed each other in opposite directions. One of the locomotives was driven by Stephenson himself.

Meanwhile, a non-passenger railway opened with far less fanfare. The Monkland & Kirkintilloch Railway, a coal-shifting rival to the Garnkirk & Glasgow, had two locomotives in operation shortly before the G&G's grand opening. The small engines, which ran at

4 to 5mph, were built by local firm Murdoch & Aitken, and were the first locomotives to be made in Glasgow. In 1832 Johnston & McNab produced another workhorse engine, the *Glasgow*. From these modest beginnings, the city's locomotive industry grew to dominate the world.

The G&G did not attract many passengers and operated on a shoestring. But they kept adding engines (especially as Stephenson's pair were troublesome) and by 1839 they had a total of six.

'Railway fever' gripped the nation from the late 1830s. The Edinburgh & Glasgow Railway opened its route between the two cities in February 1842, carrying 205,000 passengers in the first four and a half months. In June of the same year 600 members of the Glasgow Mechanics' Institution set off on a twenty-three-coach train for a half-price day trip to Edinburgh. This may have been the first organised 'excursion' in railway history.

BUILDING THE RAILWAYS

Rail passengers arriving at Queen Street station will be familiar with the long Cowlairs Tunnel just before the train comes alongside the platform. On New Year's Day 1842 the Edinburgh & Glasgow Railway opened their brand-new tunnel to the public, with hundreds queueing all day for the Grand Promenade. The crowd entered from North Queen Street and, having viewed the gaslit and whitewashed cavern, complete with its innovative telegraph, departed on Dundas Street. The announcement noted that, 'Policemen will be stationed to prevent the entrance of disorderly persons.' So great was the demand that a second promenade took place a couple of days later.

The tunnel had taken two and a half years to create and involved the excavation of 280,000 cubic yards of rock. It was on an incline so for many years trains were pulled up by a winding wire, the Cowlairs Rope, attached to the front of the engine. Trains coming down were slowed by small manned brake cars replacing the engine, which sometimes made for hair-raising moments as the brake-pads smoked and the sparks flew from the grinding blocks.

In 1911 an express from Edinburgh came down the incline too fast and ploughed through the buffers at Queen Street, its front coming to a halt just before the tables in the refreshment room, and narrowly missing the Lord Provost, Sir Archibald McInnes Shaw. Despite the speed and the damage, there were only seven injuries, all minor.

In 1841 John McCabe, an Irish navvie working on the Glasgow–Edinburgh line, fatally assaulted his English ganger (foreman). After going on the run for two months he was brought to trial in Glasgow and transported for life. Later that year two more Irish labourers, Dennis Doolan and Patrick Redding, murdered their ganger, John Green. They were not hanged at the usual place of execution on Jail Square, but taken on a cart the 6 miles to Springburn where they died facing the murder site.

Early Victorian Glasgow was a confusion of several rival railway companies running different routes and stations, all trying to better their opponents. In 1847 the first London to Glasgow East Coast route opened, although it did involve the passengers disembarking to take ferries over the Humber and the Tyne. The same year the first West Coast train arrived, with the passengers actually being brought the final 55 miles from Beattock Summit by stagecoach. By 1848 the Glasgow rail network was more-or-less complete and connected, but for many years afterwards passengers from Carlisle and the west had to disembark at Bridge Street south of the river.

By the end of the century Glasgow had four principal termini: St Enoch (opened in 1876), Central (opened in 1897 to replace Bridge Street), Buchanan Street (opened in 1849 to serve the

north), and the earliest, Queen Street, for trains to Edinburgh. These days only Central and Queen Street remain, the other two being stations on the subway.

St Enoch Hotel was the largest hotel in Scotland and the third largest in Britain, after the Langham and Midland Grand hotels in London. St Enoch station was the first building in Glasgow to be lit by electricity.

Changes in railway practice have seen the loss of many local stations. The Gorbals station closed in 1928. Bridge Street, the former terminus, vanished in 1971. Eglinton Street station went seven years earlier. Stations at Pollokshields, Shields Road and Shields combined to form the new Shields Road station in 1925. Cumberland Street station closed in 1966. There are 'ghost stations' at the Botanic Gardens and at Glasgow Cross (beneath Trongate and London Road).

BUILDING THE TRAINS

In the nineteenth century Springburn became the centre of locomotive manufacture for the British Empire. The Hyde Park Locomotive Works, for example, were turning out 300 engines a year, and the Caledonian and North British Railways and other companies also had immense manufactures close by.

In 1890 85 per cent of all locomotives in Britain were built in Glasgow.

Neilson & Co. built the *Rurik*, an 'ice engine' designed to travel over ice from St Petersburg to Kronstadt. It had steel runners shaped like large skates, and ice-spikes on the driving wheels.

Another Neilson product was the 'Connor' locomotive, exhibited in London in 1851. The huge engine was bought on the spot by Said Pasha, the Viceroy of Egypt. It ran for 35 years in Egypt, and appeared on a stamp issued in 1935 during the International Railway Congress in Cairo.

Several Glasgow-built steam locomotives are still working in India.

In 1903 several companies (including Neilson's) amalgamated into the North British Locomotive Company (NBL). During the First World War NBL sent 695 locomotives to the war area, and converted part of their Springburn premises to munitions, turning out 497,125 shells, 6,000 sea mines, 82 sets of double revolving torpedo tubes, huge numbers of trench howitzer carriages and several single-engined aircraft, plus the Mark VIII heavy tank. One of the visitors to see the tanks being tested was Winston Churchill, then Minister of Munitions.

TRAINS ON THE STREETS

For most of the nineteenth century a private railway ran down the centre of West Street in Tradeston. Owned by industrialist William Dixon, it transported coal from his colliery in Little Govan to the Coal Quay, from where it was taken downriver to his glassworks at Dumbarton. The timber tramway ran through Kingston and along the road on the east side of Springfield. The Coal Quay later became a ferry jetty.

Before the Neilson company moved close to Springburn's network of tracks, their locomotives had to taken to the railhead through the streets of central Glasgow. Low-loader trailers drawn by thirty horses thundered up West Nile Street, to the delight of small boys – although one fell under the wheels and was crushed to death.

Some locomotives for the export market were too large for the British tracks, and so were taken by road from Springburn down to Glasgow docks, their boilers sheeted with rubber to protect them from accidental contact with tram wires. Some of these engines were over 100 tons in weight even without their transporting trailer, and one sank through the road surface and burst a water main.

Glasgow companies delivered several state-of-the-art locomotives to the London International Exhibition of 1851. From the King's

Cross/Euston railhead they were pulled to South Kensington by a traction engine whose noise frightened horses so much that the operation had to take place after dark. Seeing a huge locomotive loom out of the night-time fog on the streets of London must have been an eerie sight.

BLOOD ON THE TRACKS

For decades engines had no protective cabs and drivers wore leather gauntlets and helmets to protect them from the weather. Rain in the eyes made driving almost impossible and hailstones could make the face bleed.

One of first fatal railway accidents in the world took place on 19 May 1845, when the 7.30 p.m. service from Queen Street hit a stationary train on the Edinburgh side of Gogar, killing the single passenger. Wine merchant Thomas Cooley had hired a private train from Glasgow in an attempt to make the coach from Edinburgh to Newcastle. William Paton, Superintendent of Locomotives at the Edinburgh & Glasgow Railway, and Richard McNab, the driver of the stationary train, were jailed for twelve and nine months respectively.

In 1867 Prince Alfred travelled to Glasgow to unveil a statue of Prince Albert in George Square. As the Royal Train was approaching Cowlairs West Junction, a mineral train from Sighthill to Bowling cut right across its path. The driver of the Royal Train, Jack Rennie, managed to brake to a halt less than a yard from the coal wagon rattling in front of him.

In 1903 a train arriving at St Enoch from Ardrossan crashed into the buffers at 10mph, killing sixteen. Several people died in a crash inside the Cowlairs Tunnel in 1928.

LIFE ON THE RAILWAYS

Early rail journeys were hardly the last word in comfort. Third class carriages had no seats, handrails or roof – they were just open boxes on wheels.

On one journey the smoke from the engine set fire to domestic furniture and feather beds piled in an open carriage immediately behind the tender. Frantic passengers in the third class box tried to signal the engineman, but to no avail. Only when the train stopped at Castlecary for refuelling were the flames doused by a water column.

Sparks from locomotive smoke were a constant fire hazard. At one point a Glasgow-based railway company were paying out £2,000 a year in compensation for fire damage to lineside properties.

On a Saturday in 1899 every employee and relative connected with the Caledonian Railway took a day trip to Carlisle – 14 trains, 250 carriages, 15,000 people. It was probably the largest single number of Scots to have crossed the border since Bonnie Prince Charlie's army in 1745. The heavily subsidised return fare was one shilling, and Carlisle welcomed their visitors with musical recitals, processions, bands, dancing, and cafés and hotels open all day. For years afterwards many Springburn residents dated events from the Carlisle excursion.

On Hogmanay all the locomotives in Springburn would set off their whistles at midnight, the shrieks mixing with detonators spaced at intervals along the track and exploded in coordinated patterns.

Springburn's railway heritage has almost entirely vanished. Memories and artefacts can be found in the splendid Springburn Community Museum.

GOING UNDERGROUND

The Glasgow Underground, originally called the Glasgow District Subway, was the second subterranean public transport system built in Britain after the London Underground.

The underground runs in both directions on an oval loop 6½ miles long, with fifteen stations in the city centre, the West End, and south of the Clyde. It runs on 4ft narrow gauge tracks rather than standard gauge.

After five years' work the first train left Govan at 5.00 a.m. on 14 December 1896. 25,000 people took advantage of the first day's reduced one penny fare, swamping the stations. There were several minor accidents, including the St Enoch stationmaster being pushed onto the lines by the crowd, disorder requiring police intervention, and a collision between two trains in a tunnel between Buchanan Street and St Enoch. The next day the subway was closed, reopening five weeks later once the initial troubles had been sorted out.

The trains were not electrified, but hauled by a moving cable that was kept at a continuous speed of 13mph by a coal-fired power station on Scotland Street. Each train was fitted with a gripper mechanism to grip the cable, the mechanism being released as the driver approached a station. Each of the two wire rope cables weighed 57 tons.

As they did not conduct electricity, the cables functioned even when a burst water main flooded the tunnels. The service only stopped when the water came over the floorboards of the carriages.

The cable sometimes struggled with the gradient between Govan and Partick. One train, overloaded with aggressive football fans, stopped dead in the tunnel. Some of the fans invaded the driver's cab and threatened his life unless he got things moving. Thankfully he managed to persuade them to get out and walk up the tunnel to the station, the football hordes being followed by the empty train – and a mightily relieved driver.

On 14 December 1894 thirteen workmen constructing the tunnel under the Clyde were trapped by a fire. Imprisoned for twelve hours before being rescued, they only survived by lying beneath the thickest of the smoke and passing a small airpipe from mouth to mouth. A later fire at Govan killed two men.

Because of the danger of fire the trains could not be lit by gas or paraffin lamps, and carried electric lighting cables on their superstructure.

The subway company could not make the operation pay, and sold it to Glasgow Corporation in 1922 for £385,000 – just 5 per cent of the original investment. The cable finally vanished in 1935, replaced by electrified tracks. At the same time the subway was rebranded as the Glasgow Underground.

The tunnels were not used as air raid shelters in the Second World War because they were too shallow. Partick station was bombed on 1 September 1940, both tunnels being breached and the damage taking four months to repair. Despite this, the underground was a popular way to travel because it was unaffected by wartime blackout regulations.

When the underground closed in 1977 for modernisation, it was still running the original rolling stock, the oldest such vehicles still in use anywhere in the world. When the system reopened in 1980 its new colour scheme meant it was promptly dubbed the Clockwork Orange. There was one thing everybody said they missed from the old trains – the smell.

During the refurbishment a seam of top quality coal was discovered beneath St George's Cross station. Over five months workmen used their lunch breaks to load 16 tons' worth of coal into sacks. What remains of the seam now lies beneath the station's foundations.

During 2007–8, the system saw 14.45 million journeys.

The Clockwork Orange is now no longer orange – the trains have the maroon and cream livery of the Strathclyde Partnership for Transport (SPT). And its name has reverted back to 'the subway'.

The oldest underground railway in Glasgow is actually the sub-surface suburban route between High Street and Charing Cross, opened by the Glasgow City & District Railway in 1863. Parts of the suburban Argyle railway line also run mostly underground between Finnieston West, Glasgow Central, and Dalmarnock.

TRAMS

For residents over a certain age, the much-loved trams are greatly missed. Glasgow had one of the most extensive tramway systems of any European city, covering over 100 route-miles.

The first public tramway ran in 1872 between St George's Cross and Eglinton Toll via the city centre. It was initially operated by the Glasgow Tramway and Omnibus Company, with the council taking over the system in 1894, thus creating the world's first municipal tram system.

The first trams were horse-drawn. Electrification came in from 1898 onwards. Most of the 1,000+ trams were double-deckers, some with open tops.

In the early 1960s Glasgow had the penultimate remaining tram system in Britain. The final trams were bid an emotional farewell on 4 September 1962.

Several superb examples of the old trams can be explored in the Riverside Transport Museum.

FERRIES AND STEAMERS

Ferries have been crossing the Clyde for centuries. Before the subway, most journeys across the Clyde were taken by ferry. This is the list of routes operating in 1884:

North Side	South Side
York Street	West Street
Clyde Street	Entrance to Kingston Dock
Hydepark Street	Foot of Springfield Quay
Finnieston Street	Mavisbank Quay
Kelvinhaugh Street	Maxwell St, Govan
Partick Wharf	Water Row, Govan

From 1884 to 1903 Clutha Ferries ran a half hourly service from Victoria Bridge and Broomielaw Quay to Whiteinch, bringing commuting workers from the East End and the city centre to the shipyards, engineering workshops and docks. The subway (opened in 1896) and the tram system (introduced in 1901) brought about the demise of most of the commuter ferries.

Passenger trips 'doon the watter' to Clydeside and West Coast resorts were a central part of many holidays for ordinary Glaswegians, with the Broomielaw overflowing with people and ships during Glasgow Fortnight. The very first steam-driven passenger paddle-boat in Britain sailed between Greenock and Glasgow in 1812.

On 18 September 1940 the cruiser HMS *Sussex* was badly damaged and set on fire by a 250lb bomb while it was moored at Yorkhill Quay. The surrounding area was evacuated for fear that the warship's magazine of shells would explode. *Sussex* was partially scuttled, and the fire brought under control with the assistance of the Govan ferry, which was pressed into service as an emergency fire-fighting tender for the firecrews and hoses.

At present the only operating ferry on the Clyde takes 150,000 people a year between Renfrew and Yoker. This route is actually the oldest still operating ferry service in Europe. A river bus also operates in the summer, linking Braehead, the Science Centre at Pacific Quay, and the Broomielaw in the centre.

FLIGHT

Percy Pilcher, an assistant lecturer in Naval Architecture at the University of Glasgow, was flying hang gliders at Cardross on the banks of the Clyde from the summer of 1895, the first series of repeated heavier-than-air flights in the UK.

A former RAF base, Glasgow airport was sold by the city to the British Airports Authority in 1975. Strictly speaking geographically, the airport is in Paisley/Renfrew, not Glasgow.

An average of 237 flights take off daily, serving destinations in the Scottish Islands, the rest of the UK, Europe and North America. In 2009, 7.2 million people flew in or out of Glasgow airport. Around 10 per cent of flights were delayed by more than 30 minutes.

Britain's first seaplane airline runs services from the Glasgow Science Centre to Oban and Tobermory on the Isle of Mull. This is Europe's only seaplane service operating from a city centre.

THE CHIEF DIFFICULTY TO BE OVERCOME IN AVIATION IS THAT OF RENEWING SUPPLIES OF PETROL WHILE IN THE AIR.

6

FOOD & DRINK

FOOD PRODUCTION

Thomson's Bakery at Crossmyloof may have been the largest bread-making operation in nineteenth-century Britain, producing 43,000 large loaves a day. Erected in 1847 partly to assist the local unemployed, it had 26 large ovens, consumed 500 sacks of flour a week, and had hundreds of staff.

Another large-scale operation was Buchanan's confectionery factory on Stewart Street in Cowcaddens. Glasgow's equivalent of Willy Wonka's had sugar mills, and rooms devoted to peel-making, preserves, fondant and gum goods, and lozenges.

Home-baking of 'sour cakes' was a longstanding tradition at Draigle Dubbs fair in Rutherglen. Old women gathered in the Thistle Inn or a private house and sat around in a semi-circle around the hearth. Each kneaded the dough on a knee-held bake-board, handing it from one to another again and again until it was wafer-thin. The leader, known as the 'queen', then baked the dough on a griddle. The ritual was said to be hundreds of years old.

In the sixteenth century each citizen who kept a cow had the animal looked after in common by the town's herdsman. In 1589 one John Templeton was appointed as the herdsman for all cattle north of Glasgow Cross, while John Hair was responsible for 'the nolt and guids beneath the Cross and the rest of the nether parts of the town'.

When Giffnock Quarries became worked out in the 1950s the huge caverns were used for a mushroom farm.

FOOD CONSUMPTION

Numerous reports have concluded that Glasgow's notorious ill-health is partly due to a standard diet that is high in deep-fried and over-sugared foods.

In 2004 a study by NHS Greater Glasgow found that 22 per cent of Scottish takeaways sold deep-fried Mars bars. Deep-fried pizzas were also common. The first report of a Mars bar cooked in batter appeared in 1995.

Chicken tikka masala, Britain's most popular dish, was invented in Glasgow in the late 1960s. 'Tikka' is a Bangladeshi term for marinated chicken cooked in a clay oven called a tandoor. The standard legend is that a customer in a Glaswegian tandoori asked for gravy over his chicken and the chef improvised with tomato soup, cream and spices. 'Masala' means a mix of spices. Although one in seven curries sold in Britain are 'CTMs', there is no standard recipe. When *The Real Curry Guide* tested 40 examples, they found there was only one common ingredient – chicken.

Rab Ha', a nineteenth-century celebrity known as 'the Glasgow glutton', once ate an entire calf.

FOOD MARKETS

Prior to 1755 Candleriggs was the location for the fish market, while fruit, vegetables and herbs were sold at the Greens Market on Trongate. Over the following century both markets relocated several times, with the fish market finally pitching up on Bridegate and fruit and veg eventually returning to Trongate.

In late Victorian times boxes of fish were also on sale at Queens Street goods station, where the catch was unloaded from the trains.

In 1969 the new Fruit, Vegetable and Flower Market was built on the site of the former Blochairn Steelworks, just off the M8. The building now houses 81 units employing more than 600 people, and accommodates over 2,000 vehicles a day, with customers and suppliers from the North of Scotland to mainland Europe. With an annual goods turnover in excess of £250 million, it is one of the largest horticultural markets in the UK.

The fish market followed to Blochairn in 1977 and is the only inland wholesale fish market in Scotland.

ADAM'S ALE

Fresh water originally came from a number of wells. One well on Trongate had two spouts, but only one was used. Despite the fact that both spouts drew from the same source, the local population fervently believed that drinking from the 'bad' spout would result in instant death.

The clear water of the Borgie well near Cambuslang was supposed to addle the wits. This, at least, was the story told to visitors by locals who drank from it every day.

It soon became obvious that the overworked and increasingly polluted wells could not provide the city's needs. In 1859 a massive engineering project brought fresh water from Loch Katrine in the Trossachs, giving Glasgow what was then the finest urban water supply in the country, if not the world. Many other reservoirs have now been brought into service.

Nine water storage towers dominate several parts of the city, including Bishopbriggs, Drumchapel, Cranhill and Garthamlock, where they resemble H.G. Wells' Martian spacecraft striding over the landscape.

TEA AND COFFEE

Glasgow's first coffee shop was set up at the corner of Trongate and Saltmarket by Colonel Walter Whiteford in 1678. It later became a book auction room.

Glasgow's widespread problems with drunkenness led to attempts to promote alternatives, which the pubs saw as a serious threat to their business. In 1890 the *Victualling Trades Review* condemned the terrible scourge of 'coffee drunkenness', an abominable condition for which the only cure was a nip of brandy, as provided by your local publican.

Establishments such as Miss Cranston's Willow Tea Rooms, still in existence on Sauchiehall Street, were set up so that women (and men) could meet socially without having to consume alcohol.

ALCOHOL

The town council of the seventeenth century kept the local aristocrats sweet with gifts of wine. The Earl of Argyle, for example received seventeen gallons at a time.

In 1668 the city spent 160 Scots pounds on a hogshead of wine (a hogshead was 46 gallons or 209 litres). The wine was consumed on Communion Sunday, at a time when communicants took rather more than the present-day sip.

In 1705 the council imposed a tax of two pennies on every pint of ale brewed and sold in the town. Having thus raised £3,600 Scots (£300 Sterling), they funded solicitor and antiquarian James Anderson in his survey of ancient charters. Why the ale-drinkers of Glasgow should be called upon specifically to bankroll such a project was a question never raised.

Robert and Hugh Tennent founded Wellpark Brewery at Drygate in 1740. By the mid-nineteenth century J. & R. Tennent was the world's largest exporter of bottled beer. Its current bestselling brand is Tennent's Lager.

When a snake was found in a cargo of hides sent from South America to a chemical works, the manager bottled it in spirits. Taking it on the train to the Kelvingrove

Museum, he met two farmers, who asked how the reptile had been killed. On replying that he had drowned it in whisky, one farmer turned to the other and said, 'Ay, man, sic a glorious death!'

An illegal still was set up in West Nile Street during the Second World War, a time when whisky was restricted and expensive. The home-made distilling operation was discovered when the operation accidentally set the building on fire.

Maryhill had the first Temperance Society in Britain, founded in 1829.

PUBS

As is usual, there is disagreement about which of Glasgow's existing pubs is the oldest. A good candidate is the Scotia Bar in Stockwell Street, built in 1792.

The Saracen's Head Inn on Gallowgate was built in 1755 by Robert Tennent using stones scavenged from the ruined Bishop's Castle next to the cathedral. In 1782 'the Surprising Irish Giant' was exhibited here, a twenty-one-year-old who was supposedly 8ft tall. The present 'Sarrie Heid' is not on the same site and shares just the name with its predecessor. Built in 1905, it holds a blunderbuss carried for protection on the London coach, and a polished skull found when digging a former graveyard on the site.

The oldest pub in Byres Road is the Curlers Rest. Its predecessor was built beside a curling pond, and it may have been in existence since the seventeenth century.

The Black Bull on Argyle Street became the fashionable hostelry for Glasgow's smart set. In 1761 the body of Archibald, the Duke of Argyle, lay in state for several days in the inn, awaiting its departure to the family vault in Kilmun.

The Hangman's Rest, which used to stand on Wilson Street, had a 'real' noose, and murals (later, decorated windows) showing the gallows tree. The pub's name, which is much disputed, may have come from the time when the local executioner, who was shunned in the city centre pubs, was welcomed here.

Many connoisseurs regard the Old Toll Bar on Paisley Road Toll as possessing the finest nineteenth-century pub interior in Glasgow. The exterior is less impressive because the Victorian stained-glass windows were all smashed during the Glasgow Rent Strike of 1915.

It is alleged that when the Stone of Destiny was stolen from Westminster Abbey in 1950, it was briefly stored in the cellar of the New Arlington Pub on Woodlands Road.

In 1831, when Glasgow was a fraction of today's size, the city contained 2,850 pubs and about half that number of brothels.

Many of the twentieth-century dispersed housing schemes had no pub because of the city's policy on 'dry' wards. The massive estate of Castlemilk, for example, had no licensed premises until the 1980s.

7

CITY OF CULTURE

Glasgow was declared the European City of Culture for 1990.

MOVIELAND GLASGOW

In 2010 the *Independent* described Glasgow as 'Britain's second film-making hub, after London.'

During 2008, 181 film and television productions were shot in Glasgow, including over 20 feature films or full-length dramas, bringing over £17 million into the local economy. Part of this success can be attributed to the opening in 2009 of Film City Glasgow, a purpose-built production facility in the former Govan Town Hall.

Several short-lived film companies worked in Glasgow during the silent era. The first version of *Rob Roy* was filmed in a former tram depot in Rouken Glen in 1911. The filmmakers' electricity supply, which was still connected to the tramways, fluctuated in time with the movement of the distant trams. Over in Thornliebank, The Ace Film Producing Company made just one feature, *The Harp King* (1919).

Scottish Film Productions, set up in India Street in 1928, specialised in non-feature films such as shorts, newsreels and documentaries. In 1936 the first edition of *Things That Happen,* their monthly magazine-film for Glasgow cinemas, opened with footage of what was said to be the Loch Ness Monster. Many years later the cameraman admitted the shots had been faked – on Loch Lomond.

Madeleine (1949), directed by David Lean, told the story of the alleged poisoning by Madeleine Smith of her lover Emile L'Angelier in 1857. Some of it was filmed in Blythswood Square, the scene of the actual events.

Ronnie Corbett made his screen debut in *You're Only Young Twice* (1953), a comedy about the election for the Rector of the University of Glasgow. Some of it was filmed on location at Gilmorehill.

In the Ealing Studios comedy *The Maggie* (1954), the disreputable puffer of the title sails up the Clyde without proper guidance and strikes the tunnel of the Glasgow Underground. One of the characters gets to say the line, 'You say a boat is stuck on the subway?'

The Necropolis, Finnieston and the West End all appeared in the moody and dystopian European science fiction film *Death Watch* (1980, also known as *La Mort en direct*). Director Bertrand Tavernier picked Glasgow over Berlin because it fitted his vision of a bleak future. Harvey Keitel plays a journalist with a camera implanted in his eye so he can secretly film a terminally ill woman for a reality TV show. Look out for an early appearance by Robbie Coltrane.

Doomsday (2008) is an unpleasant future of an altogether different stripe, with cannabilistic crazies running loose over recognisable landmarks in a post-apocalyptic Glasgow.

Urban Ghost Story (1998) is a kind of street version of *The Exorcist*, in which a 12-year-old girl living in a grim Glasgow high-rise is plagued by a poltergeist.

More gritty urban realism can be found in the 'grotcore' films *Ratcatcher* (1999) and *Red Road* (2006), while 'hard man' themes about Glaswegian working-class male violence and culture are picked out in *Silent Scream* (1989), *The Big Man* (1990), *The Near Room* (1995), *Small Faces* (1996) and *The Acid House* (1998).

A Sense of Freedom (1981), based on the autobiography of murderer-turned-artist Jimmy Boyle, caused considerable controversy. Boyle's long-held reputation for violence meant that the Scottish Prison Service refused to cooperate, so the scenes set in Barlinnie prison were filmed in Dublin.

Glasgow has provided locations for many a comedy, from *The Girl in the Picture* (1985), starring John Gordon Sinclair as a lovelorn photographer, to hairdressing film *The Big Tease* (1999), *Beautiful Creatures* (2000 – think a Scottish *Thelma & Louise*), the 2002 Danish-UK co-production *Wilbur Wants to Kill Himself* (set in a second-hand bookshop), slacker-fest *Late Night Shopping* (2001), whose locations included the Clyde Tunnel, and *American Cousins* (2003), which brings New Jersey mobsters to an Italian fish and chip shop in Glasgow.

Glasgow's great advantage for film-making is the variety of locations it can offer. *Young Adam* (2003) was filmed on the Forth & Clyde and Union Canals. *O Lucky Man!* (1973) and *This Is Not A Love Song* (2002) included scenes at Barlinnie prison. Martial arts epic *Unleashed* (2005, also known as *Danny the Dog*) charged through Broomhill Shopping Centre, Kelvingrove Museum, and the Botanic Gardens.

REEL LIFE

In 1914 James Hart, the manager of the Grosvenor Cinema off Byres Road, filmed Edwardian West End Glasgow in its pomp, as the churches emptied of their well-dressed congregations on a Sunday afternoon on Great Western Road. Hart attempted to reshoot the same sequence in 1922, but the impact of the First World War was evident – the crowds were smaller, the Sunday outfits less demonstrative, and most tellingly, very few young men were to be seen.

Another significant Glasgow short was the fifteen-minute *Dear Green Place* (1960), which consisted of evocative black-and-white photographs set to the songs of folk singer Ewan McColl.

At a time when 'industrial' documentaries were still made as supporting films for mainstream movies, awards were bestowed on *Seawards the Great Ships* (1961), which celebrated Clyde shipbuilding, and *The Big Mill* (1963), a study of the steelworks at Ravenscraig and Gartcosh.

GLASGOW SUBSTITUTING FOR OTHER PLACES ON SCREEN

The interior scenes and many of the exterior locations for the Edinburgh-set films *Shallow Grave* (1994) and *Trainspotting* (1996) were actually filmed in Glasgow. The same was the case for the gritty thriller *The Debt Collector* (1999), starring Billy Connolly and Ken Stott.

In *Man Dancin'* (2003) Glasgow substituted for Belfast.

The gorgeous interior of the City Chambers has proved to be a very adaptable location. For religious comedy *Heavenly Pursuits* (1986) it was the Vatican, three years earlier the building masqueraded as the Kremlin for *An Englishman Abroad,* about the spy Guy Burgess, and in 2000 it appeared as an early twentieth-century New York mansion in *The House of Mirth*. Further locations for this period drama included Kelvingrove Museum and the Theatre Royal. The City Chambers is also briefly seen in the gangster flick *The Long Good Friday* (1979).

The Vogue bingo hall in Riddrie, a former cinema, was used for a London setting in *Silent Scream* (1989).

Somewhat remarkably, The Barras market featured in *Restless Natives* (1985) – as New Mexico.

AND OTHER PLACES PRETENDING TO BE GLASGOW

The Gorbals Story (1949) was actually filmed in London.

CINEMA STORIES

The first film ever shown in Glasgow (and only the second in Scotland) was projected at a skating rink on Sauchiehall Street on 25 May 1896. The short silent was screened using the Lumière projection system. A few years earlier the entertainment venue had been pulling the crowds in with a painted panorama of the Battle of Bannockburn.

The Salon Cinema in Hillhead was one of the first buildings in Britain constructed specifically as a cinema (as distinct from adapting an existing place of entertainment).

The 1938 Empire Exhibition saw a specially constructed Empire Cinema rise in Bellahouston Park. It screened documentaries about Scotland, including three with significant scenes filmed in Glasgow – *Wealth of a Nation*, *The Children's Story* and *The Face of Scotland*. After the exhibition the cinema was dismantled and reconstructed at Lochgilphead in Argyll (it is now the Empire Travel Lodge).

The Cosmo on Rose Street, opened in 1939, was the first Scottish cinema dedicated largely to foreign language and non-Hollywood films – in other words, it was Scotland's earliest 'arthouse' cinema. It now operates on similar lines, renamed as the Glasgow Film Theatre, a highly successful regional film centre.

FILM DIRECTORS

George T. Miller, who directed the 1982 Australian film *The Man From Snowy River*, emigrated from Glasgow in the 1940s.

Alexander Mackendrick studied painting at Glasgow School of Art, leaving without a degree in 1929. He went on to direct the classic films *The Ladykillers*, *The Man in the White Suit*, *Sweet Smell of Success*, *The Maggie*, *Whisky Galore!* and *A High Wind in Jamaica*. He was actually born in Boston, Massachusetts because his Glaswegian parents had eloped to America to flee family disapproval.

Director Ken Loach has often used Glasgow as the setting for nuanced studies of ordinary people in crisis, including *Riff-Raff* (1990), *Carla's Song* (1996), *My Name is Joe* (1998), *Sweet Sixteen* (2002) and *Ae Fond Kiss . . .* (2004). Glasgow films of a similar genre include *On a Clear Day* (2005) and *AfterLife* (2003).

Several of Loach's films star the instantly recognisable Peter Mullan, who has directed his own critically acclaimed (and controversy-creating) films *Orphans* (1997), *The Magdalene Sisters* (2002) and *Neds* (2010).

A gentler view of Glasgow life at the sharp end is portrayed in Bill Forsyth's comedy *That Sinking Feeling* (1980), which was the first feature-length film made entirely in Scotland (other than those productions sponsored by the government or official organisations). The director's third comedy (after the Cumbernauld-set *Gregory's Girl*) was *Comfort and Joy* (1984), the tale of a Glaswegian disc jockey becoming involved in a turf dispute over ice-cream van routes. In a grim coincidence, after the film was completed but before it was released, a real-life (and very violent) ice-cream gang war broke out in the city.

ACTORS AND ACTRESSES

Stan Laurel – of Laurel and Hardy fame – was brought up in Glasgow.

Glasgow-born Mary Gordon (1882–1963) often appeared as Basil Rathbone's housekeeper Mrs Hudson in the *Sherlock Holmes* films, and turned up with Laurel and Hardy in the 1935 film *Bonnie Scotland*.

Gordon Jackson (1923–90) was a distinguished character actor who appeared in more than 80 films; many viewers from the 1970s will remember him as the butler Angus Hudson in the television period drama *Upstairs, Downstairs*, or as the head of the secret service CI5 in *The Professionals*.

David McCallum was born in Glasgow in 1933. Depending on your vintage, you will know him as 1960s secret agent Illya Kuryakin in *The Man From U.N.C.L.E.*, 1980s interdimensional traveller in *Sapphire and Steel,* or, from 2003, as an irascible medical examiner in *NCIS*.

Richard Wilson was a research scientist at Stobhill Hospital before becoming an actor. His iconic roles have included Mr Clockerty in *Tutti Frutti* and Victor 'I don't believe it!' Meldrew in *One Foot in the Grave.*

Robbie Coltrane is one of the most recognisable actors in the world, not least because he plays the half-giant Hagrid in the *Harry Potter* films. He got his first screen break in the 1980 films *Deathwatch* and *Flash Gordon.*

David Hayman, best known for playing Chief Superintendent Michael Walker in the long-running *Trial & Retribution* television series, runs the Spirit Aid charity, which helps impoverished children in Malawi, Sri Lanka, Afghanistan and Glasgow.

Peter Capaldi wrote and starred in the road movie comedy *Soft Top Hard Shoulder* (1992), about a supposedly simple drive from London to Glasgow, and wrote and directed *Strictly Sinatra* (2001), a spoof Glaswegian-Italian mafiosi picture. In 1993 Capaldi made *Franz Kafka's It's a Wonderful Life*, a short comic film in which Kafka, attempting to complete his masterwork *The Metamorphosis* (a story about a man transformed into a cockroach), is constantly interrupted by ludicrous events. Made for BBC Scotland in Glasgow and starring Richard E. Grant as Kafka, it won a BAFTA for Best Short Film and an Oscar for best Live Action Short Film.

Bill Paterson sent in a short story to a Radio 4 competition under the pseudonym Tulloch Cameron. The BBC wrote to 'Mr Cameron' stating they would be delighted to broadcast it – and, to read it on air, they wanted to hire the actor Bill Paterson. The author owned up, and several more humorous reminiscences of his Dennistoun childhood were broadcast and collected in the book *Tales from the Back Green* (2008).

TV DRAMA

With BBC Scotland and STV both headquartered in Glasgow, and Channel 4 also active here, it is not surprising many memorable television dramas have been set in the city.

Many people remember the thriller serial *Brond* for the menace exuded by the actor Stratford Johns, especially the scene where the smiling villain casually tips a young lad over the side of the Kelvin Bridge on Gibson Street.

Sea of Souls was a creepy paranormal series starring Bill Paterson as the leader of the Department of Parapsychology at 'Clyde University' in the city centre.

Other BBC hits include *Takin' over the Asylum* and *Your Cheatin' Heart,* while without doubt their most famous drama was *Tutti Frutti,* a tragicomic tale of aging rock 'n' rollers written by John Byrne in 1987. It featured iconic roles for Robbie Coltrane as Danny McGlone, Emma Thompson as Suzi Kettles, Richard Wilson as Eddie Clockerty and Katy Murphy as Ms Toner.

BBC Scotland's long-running soap opera *River City* is set in the fictional town of Shieldinch, somewhere within the Glasgow boundary. The series is actually filmed in Dumbarton.

TAGGART

STV's greatest hit is without doubt *Taggart,* which has been on air since 1983, reaching 100 episodes in 2009, making it the longest-running police drama on British TV. The gritty series revolves around murder detectives based at Maryhill CID.

The original concept was as a one-off three-part detective drama, with no thought of it becoming a series. The show was called *Killer* and the Taggart name did not appear in the title. At the time, STV had no track record of making long-term police series.

Glenn Chandler, the creator of the granite-faced Glasgow detective Jim Taggart, took his character's surname from a gravestone.

The dour and bad-tempered Detective Chief Inspector Jim Taggart was played by Mark McManus, whose line 'There's been a murrrrrder' became a much-parodied catchphrase. The actor's broken nose and craggy features were the result of a total of 140 stitches he received during his career as a boxer in Australia. When not investigating an apparently endless series of mutilated corpses on screen, McManus bred butterflies. In an interview he said, 'In some pubs in Glasgow, they still dash out the back door when I come in 'cos they think I'm one of the bizzies!'

McManus played Jim Taggart from 1983 until his death in 1994. No-one was brought in to substitute for his iconic role and the lead character was killed off on screen. Despite this, the show retains the name *Taggart* as a familiar brand-name. This sometimes confuses new viewers, as there is no indication of who Taggart was.

The series continued with the detectives now led by Jim Taggart's long-suffering former sidekick, Detective Inspector (now Detective Chief Inspector) James MacPherson, played by Michael Jardine. From 2002 the lead character has been DCI Matt Burke, another 'old school' copper in the vein of Jim Taggart, played by the redoubtable Alex Norton.

Alex Norton actually had a minor role in a *Taggart* episode back in 1985, but not as a police officer.

Much of the gritty quality of the series comes from its use of real Glasgow locations, from pedestrian walkways near the M8 to the Botanic Gardens, Kelvingrove Park, the university, Pollokshields, Govan, the St Enoch Centre, grim housing schemes, subway stations, and many other places.

Taggart's boss in the first episode was Superintendent Robert Murray, known behind his back as 'The Mint' (from Murray Mint). Similarly in the later series Taggart and the others referred to their new boss, Superintendent Jack McVitie, as 'The Biscuit'.

On one occasion a group of *Taggart* extras dressed in police uniforms were on their way to a location when their coach became stuck in traffic on the M8. The actors passed the time by staring menacingly at neighbouring cars and pretending to note down details. A number of drivers were no doubt very relieved when the coach moved off.

GLASGOW'S TOP TEN FICTIONAL DETECTIVES

Apart from Jim Taggart, Glasgow has spawned a full file of fictional detectives.

1. Dick Donovan ('The Glasgow Detective') was the pseudonym used by Joyce Emmerson Preston Muddock (1842–1934) for something approaching 250 stories and 50 books. Although he was completely fictional, many people claimed to have met Dick Donovan, and, long before Sherlock Holmes received the same accolade, the Glasgow Detective was always being asked by members of the public to assist in real-life investigations. Donovan's fame is the reason why hard-boiled American detectives are called 'dicks'.

2. Detective Inspector Jack Laidlaw is very hard-boiled; he's the unsettling hero in William McIlvanney's trio of novels *Laidlaw* (1977), *The Papers of Tony Veitch* (1983) and *Strange Loyalties* (1991).

3. Craig Russell – a former Glasgow policeman – puts his shady private investigator Lennox in a neo-noir 1950s Glasgow in *Lennox* (2009), *The Long Glasgow Kiss* (2010) and *The Deep Dark Sleep* (2011).

4. Forensic scientist Rhona MacLeod has poked through blood and bone in eight grimly realistic bestselling novels since *Driftnet* in 2003. Author Lin Anderson has stated she partly modelled Rhona's acerbic friend Chrissy on *Tutti Frutti*'s Ms Toner.

5. Detective Chief Inspector William Lorimer, Alex Gray's thoughtful creation, has been hunting serial killers over eight novels since his introduction in *Never Somewhere Else* (2003).

6. Detective Inspectors Colin Thane and Phil Moss of the Glasgow-based Scottish Crime Squad can be found in twenty-four books by Bill Knox. Knox was the former presenter of the STV programme *Crime Desk*.

7. The detectives of Peter Turnbull's P Division turned out to solve numerous bloody Glasgow crimes over ten novels, starting with *Deep and Crisp and Even* in 1981.

8. Campbell Armstrong's Detective Sergeant Lou Perlman is a Jewish copper in Glasgow's East End, in *The Last Darkness* (2002), *White Rage* (2004) and *Butcher* (2006).

9. Paddy Meehan is a Glasgow journalist, not a cop, but she's soon oxter-deep in solving violent crimes in Denise Mina's trilogy *The Field of Blood* (2005), *The Dead Hour* (2006) and *The Last Breath* (2007).

10. Perhaps the most unusual Glasgow 'tec' is private investigator Derek Adams, whose speciality is the occult. *Noir* meets H.P. Lovecraft in William Meikle's *The Midnight Eye Files* trilogy.

THEATRES

The dour Protestants of the Reformation loathed public performances, which they regarded as both rife with immorality and reminiscent of the quasi-religious theatrical events of Catholic times. It was not until 1752 that a makeshift theatre appeared in Glasgow, at the top of the High Street. Attendees sometimes required armed guards to protect them from the anger of the mob. The booth was demolished in 1754 under the orders of a firebrand minister who saw the performances as 'a limb of Satan'.

The next theatre opened in 1764 in Alston Street, Grahamstown, now the area beneath the Central station but at the time a village outside the city boundaries, and hence protected from the disapproving magistrates. On the opening night the machinery and scenery were deliberately set on fire and in 1782 it finally burned to the ground.

Sheridan Knowles worked as a teacher of elocution on Trongate, writing plays in his spare time. In 1820 he sent his work *Virginius* to William Macready, one of the greatest actors of the London stage. Macready received it unwillingly, as he had had poor results with Glasgow playwrights, but as soon as he read the manuscript he took the first coach to Glasgow, where, incognito, he watched the play during its run at the Theatre Royal on Queen Street. Within a month *Virginius* was wowing the crowds at Covent Garden, and Sheridan Knowles was the toast of London theatreland.

Perhaps Glasgow's most celebrated acting emporium is the Citizens Theatre, on Main Street in Gorbals. The 'Citz' has long had a reputation for producing both challenging and popular work. In 1949–50 its pantomime *The Tintock Cup* ran for five months without a break. Many famous actors came to prominence at the Citizens, including Bill Paterson, David Hayman, Stanley Baxter, Duncan McRae, Molly Urquhart and James Gibson.

LITERARY VISITORS

Thomas De Quincey, the eccentric author of *Confessions of An English Opium-Eater,* lived at 112 Rottenrow in the 1840s. He maintained a second lodging at 79 Renfield Street, which he used exclusively as a store for his books. On leaving Glasgow he left a number of volumes and manuscripts with a local bookseller. Some years later, when he wanted his property back, De Quincey had forgotten the man's name and address, and it took great efforts by the writer's friends to locate the works.

In 1848 Charles Dickens appeared on stage at the Dunlop Street Theatre in an amateur dramatics performance of *The Merry Wives of Windsor.* The event was in essence a forerunner of the 'benefit gig', with Dickens' literary chums (the Company of London Amateurs) turning up in aid of the local unemployed and the Shakespeare House Fund. More than £68 was raised over two nights, by far the largest receipts taken during the nationwide tour.

Ten years later Dickens read his own works over three evenings and one morning at Glasgow, and took £600, one of the most profitable events of his career. Further readings were given in Glasgow in 1861, 1868, and finally in 1869, when he was very ill.

Harriet Beecher Stowe, author of *Uncle Tom's Cabin*, visited Glasgow in 1853, where she received delegations of admirers and anti-slavery campaigners from all over Scotland.

Anthony Trollope spent several months in the city during 1857–8, as part of his job as a postal surveyor. He used his experience of the Glasgow post office in his novel *The Three Clerks.*

In 1755 the Saracen's Head Inn opened on the Gallowgate, and rapidly became the fashionable place to stay for bohemian visitors. In 1764 the brothers Foulis met Thomas Gray here, and agreed to print a *de luxe* edition of the poet's works. Dr Samuel Johnson and James Boswell put up at the inn in 1773 (part of Boswell's education had been at Glasgow University). William Wordsworth, his sister Dorothy and Samuel Taylor Coleridge stayed here in 1803 (they didn't care for Glasgow – it was too busy, and it rained heavily all the time they were there).

There used to be a plaque near the Saracen's Head stating that Adam Smith was once barred from the establishment for calling Dr Johnson 'A son of a bitch'. If this ever really happened, it may be related to an exchange that took place in London: Adam Smith was boasting about the wonders of Glasgow, to which Johnson witheringly replied, 'Pray, sir, have you ever seen Brentford?'

The present 'Sarrie Heid' is not exactly on the same spot, and shares nothing with its predecessor other than the name.

NOVELISTS

Tobias Smollett was born in Dunbartonshire and apprenticed to a Saltmarket apothecary; his unloved employers, Drs Gordon and Crawford, were lampooned in *The Adventures of Roderick Random*, written in 1748.

Anthony Burgess called Alasdair Gray 'the greatest Scottish novelist since Walter Scott'. Gray's first novel, *Lanark: A Life in 4 Books*, published in 1981, is a fantasy-realist apocalyptic epic that flits between two alternative Glasgows, one of which bears a resemblance to the real city in the 1950s. His other works, all justly celebrated, include *1982 Janine, The Fall of Kelvin Walker, Poor Things, Unlikely Stories Mostly* and *A History Maker,* and are often laced with elaborate jokes, satires on Scottish life, fiction presented as real-world fact (and vice-versa), contradictory narratives, and personal appearances by someone who claims to be Alasdair Gray. The polymath Gray is also a playwright, poet and artist, often illustrating his own works.

Perhaps the first appearance of Glasgow in science fiction was in an anonymous book entitled *How Glasgow ceased to flourish: a tale of 1890*. It was published in 1884.

The magazine *Nebula Science Fiction* was produced in Glasgow from 1952 to 1959, and was the first place to publish Brian W. Aldiss, Robert Silverberg and Bob Shaw, later all giants of the genre.

More recent Glasgow-based sci-fi can be found in the anthology *Starfield*, edited by Duncan Lunan. Lunan is a member of the Glasgow Science Fiction Writers' Circle, which has produced several published authors in the field.

Professor Archie E. Roy, not content with merely being a famous astronomer and founding president of the Scottish Society for Psychical Research, wrote six novels with supernatural or occult themes, including *Devil In The Darkness* (1978) and *All Evil Shed Away* (1970), the latter including a scene in Nazi-occupied Glasgow.

The Devil turns up in Glasgow in person in Fergus Blythswood's *Satan on Holiday* (1903) – he even manages a visit to the 1901 Exhibition.

In *So I Am Glad* (1995), West End-based A.L. Kennedy places a 375-year-old Cyrano de Bergerac in a bedsit in Partick.

Catherine Carswell, born in Glasgow in 1879, was one of the most controversial women novelists of the early twentieth century, for candidly discussing sexual feelings in books such as *Open the Door* (1920).

Alistair Maclean, who was born in Glasgow but raised in Inverness-shire, became a tax exile in Switzerland after the phenomenal success of his thrillers *Where Eagles Dare, The Guns of Navarone* and *Ice Station Zebra*.

Perhaps the most famous Glasgow novel is *No Mean City* (1935) by Alexander McArthur and H. Kingsley Long. Mired in controversy over its exact authorship and its depiction of razor gangs, it has never been out of print. At one point Glasgow City Libraries refused to stock it. 'No Mean City' is the name of both an album by the rock group Nazareth and the title theme of *Taggart*.

When James Kelman's *How Late It Was, How Late*, which is rich in Glaswegian demotic, won the Booker Prize in 1994, one of the judges asked for the rules to be changed so that nothing like it could appear again in the competition.

Street vernacular, copious bodily fluids and Glaswegian locations are employed to comic and thrilling effect in Christopher Brookmyre's series of 'Tartan noir' novels. *The Sacred Art of Stealing* (2003) centres around an absurdist bank heist on Buchanan Street. *Attack of the Unsinkable Rubber Ducks* (2007), set in a barely disguised University of Glasgow, sticks the knife into fake psychics. Other targets of the author's ire include Celtic fans, Rangers fans, sectarianism, Scottish religious leaders and Scottish Tories.

SIR WALTER SCOTT

Although primarily associated with Edinburgh, the Lothians and the Borders, Scotland's most famous writer had many connections with Glasgow.

When he was still an officer of the court – before his literary fame – Scott often attended the old Court House on Jail Square (now Jocelyn Square), staying at an inn on King Street around the corner.

Scott's 1817 novel *Rob Roy* – which did much to invent the myth of the eponymous MacGregor outlaw – has many scenes set in Glasgow. It is in the atmospheric gloom of the crypt of Glasgow Cathedral that Rob Roy speaks out of the shadows to warn Francis Osbaldistone of the danger to his life; the duo meet again on Stockwell Bridge at midnight and are interviewed in a cell in the Tolbooth on Trongate; there is a quarrel in the gardens of the (now-vanished) Old College on High Street; Luckie Flyter's hostelry is placed in the Old Wynd, off Trongate; and Messrs MacVittie and MacFinn pitch up at a counting-house on the Gallowgate.

Rob Roy's most enduring creation was Bailie Nicol Jarvie, a canny merchant and couthy, cautious urbanite who gets caught up in shenanigans in the Highlands. The character of Jarvie took on a life of its own.

From 1872 *The Bailie* was the premier Glasgow social periodical, which was not only named after Nicol Jarvie, but was supposed to be edited by him. Correspondents would address their letters to 'Dear Bylie' or 'My Magistrate'. In 1922 *The Bailie* published a full biography of its supposed founder, inventing everything from his date and place of birth to accounts of his early years and education.

When Queen Victoria visited Glasgow in 1849 she was shown, at her request, Nicol Jarvie's house on Saltmarket. It stood behind the Original Bailie Nicol Jarvie Tavern, both buildings having developed their fake associations purely through the success of Scott's fiction.

Crookston Castle features in Scott's novel *The Abbot*. From the shadow of the adjacent Crookston Yew Mary, Queen of Scots views the defeat of her forces at the Battle of Langside several miles away. Unfortunately for Scott's verisimilitude, this could not have happened, as rising ground intrudes between Crookston and Langside.

A statue of Sir Walter Scott atop an 80-foot high column occupies the central position in George Square. Erected in 1837, it was the first major municipal tribute to Scott, predating Edinburgh's Scott Monument by several years.

A less conventional sculptural reminder of Scott can be found at 64 Waterloo Street. The building used to belong to United Distillers, which had a brand of whisky named Roderick Dhu, after the Romantic hero of Scott's hugely popular narrative poem 'The Lady of the Lake'. The façade is decorated with statues of Roderick, his rival James Fitzjames, and Ellen Douglas, the eponymous heroine, who is depicted beside a small waterfall, holding the paddle which helped her escape from her island prison on Loch Katrine.

GRAPHIC NOVELS AND COMICS

Glasgow hosts two giants of the graphic novel/comic medium. Grant Morrison has written for characters such as Batman, Superman, Doctor Who, Judge Dredd, The Flash, The Justice League of America, The X-Men, Fantastic Four and The Seven Soldiers. Some of *Animal Man* is set in Anniesland, while other characters have been given a Glaswegian makeover. An early work was a weekly comic strip called *Captain Clyde* (about an unemployed superhero), which appeared in *The Govan Press*.

Mark Millar (who is from Coatbridge but now lives in Glasgow), has worked on The X-Men, The Avengers, The Authority, The Fantastic Four, Judge Dredd, The Flash, Superman, Wolverine, Spiderman, Swamp Thing and many others. He is not shy of controversy, attracting criticism for his 2000AD strip *Big Dave* (co-authored with Grant Morrison), his satires of religion and politics, and the violence in his own comic *Kick-Ass*. The latter became a hit movie.

In *The Bogie Man* (1989–92) a man suffering from the delusion that he is Humphrey Bogart sets about 'solving' the plot from *The Maltese Falcon* in contemporary Glasgow. His mistaken assumptions lead to chaos and run-ins with real-life criminals and coppers, culminating in a destructive climax in Central station. Other locations are well used, including the Necropolis and the West End. Filled with allusions to *film noir* classics, the witty comic was written by Alan Grant and John Wagner.

Denise Mina brought trenchcoated demon-hunter John Constantine to Glasgow for two graphic novels in the *Hellblazer* series, with the central characters taking refuge in the Kelvingrove Museum as the apocalypse approaches.

Newspaper cartoonist Bud Neill (1911–70) created an enduring and much-loved character in Lobey Dosser, the Sheriff of Calton Creek, whose horse has only two legs. A statue of Lobey and his arch-enemy Rank Bajin was erected at the junction of Lynedoch Street and Woodlands Road in 1992. The sculpture has a key role in the plot of Christopher Brookmyre's 1999 absurdist-terrorism novel *A Big Boy Did It And Ran Away*.

POETS

Glasgow missed out on the opportunity to 'discover' Robert Burns. In 1786 Burns showed his work to William Reid, then an apprentice at Dunlop & Wilson on Trongate. Reid thought the poems were excellent, but explained that his employers did not publish poetry. Other Glasgow printers also turned down the Ayrshire bard. William Reid went on to became a partner in Brash & Reid, who later published the first significant collection of Burns' works in Glasgow.

In the 1870s a nephew of Robert Burns was held as a lunatic patient in the Govan poorhouse.

James Macfarlan was one of the first poets to celebrate the industrial working classes, with works such as 'The Lords of Labour' ('Ho! these are the Titans of toil and trade / The heroes who wield no sabre / But mightier conquests reapeth the blade / Which is borne by the Lords of Labour'). An alcoholic, he died in poverty in 1862, aged thirty-one.

Another industrial poet was Alexander Smith, whose 'Glasgow' (1857) includes the line, 'Instead of shores where ocean beats / I hear the ebb and flow of streets'. Another quote from Smith – 'A sacredness of love and death / Dwells in thy noise and smoky breath' – can be found inscribed at 77 Queen Street (his former place of employment), to the right of the entrance to South Exchange Court.

In 1810 James Hogg, then one of Scotland's most eminent writers, travelled from Edinburgh to Paisley just to meet Robert Tannahill. When Hogg arrived he asked for Tannahill the poet, but none of the Paisley people knew of him. Eventually Hogg found the poet working at a weaving loom.

Robert Tannahill.

Shortly afterwards Tannahill, who was suffering from a mental illness, drowned himself in the River Cart. He was thirty-six.

Glaswegian poet William Motherwell (1797–1835) drank himself to death.

Poet Ellen Johnston worked as a power-loom weaver from the age of ten and died in a Glasgow poorhouse when she was thirty-eight.

Edwin Muir's entire family died after moving from Orkney to Glasgow, and his own health suffered badly.

Schoolteacher John Wilson (1720–89) eulogised Scotstoun and Blythswood in his poem 'The Clyde'. When he moved from Rutherglen to the grammar school at Greenock, his new employers specified that he give up 'the profane and unprofitable art of poem-making', an edict which broke his spirit.

In the early nineteenth century Kelvin Grove was a wooded dell some 2 miles outside the city, where young people would stroll and picnic on Sunday afternoons. 'Kelvin Grove', a song celebrating this trysting place ('Let us haste to Kelvin Grove, bonnie lassie o') became very famous. Through a series of editing mistakes it was attributed to John Sim. After Sim died, Glasgow-based doctor Thomas Lyle (1792–1859) proved his own authorship, so a music seller who had licensed the song from Sim's estate had to renegotiate the copyright with Lyle.

The abiding nursery rhyme 'Wee Willie Winkie' was written by Glasgow man William Miller.

Edwin Morgan (1920–2010) was *the* Glasgow poet, his collection *The Second Life* (1968) being known to many. In 2004 he was named as Scotland's first national poet, the Scots Makar. In 2002 he collaborated with the rock band Idlewild on their album *The Remote Part*, reciting a specially written poem, 'Scottish Fiction'.

WRITERS' LIVES

Christopher North, who achieved fame at *Blackwood's Magazine* in Edinburgh, was the pseudonym of John Wilson, who left his native Paisley at the age of twelve to attend Glasgow University. He recalled how a man named Mr Douglas, of Glasgow, was so offended by a piece in the magazine that he took a coach to Edinburgh and struck Mr Blackwood a single time with his horsewhip. The publisher gathered another whip, pursued Mr Douglas to the departing coach, and beat him severely until the vehicle sped away.

In the eighteenth century the Literary and Commercial Society (distinguished members: Adam Smith, David Hume, Edmund Burke and the Foulis brothers) regularly met at the Black Bull, a hostelry on Argyle Street that was also frequented by the Gaelic Club and Robert Burns. The Black Bull was one of the few places where 'gentlemen' could drink and dine without too much annoyance by the riff-raff.

PRINTING

A pioneering print-shop was set up by George Anderson in 1638, although the first book printed in Glasgow did not appear until the following year – *Catechisms* by Zachary Boyd, a local minister.

Like Boyd's book most of the earliest works printed in Glasgow were exclusively religious in character (and Protestant, of course).

The early Glasgow printers do not appear to have been of the highest quality; as late as 1713 academics at the university were obliged to send off to Edinburgh for reprinted and corrected pages.

In 1718 James Duncan set up as a typefounder in Saltmarket and printed McUre's *History of Glasgow*, the first attempt to tell the complete story of Glasgow's past.

The great Glasgow publishing success was Collins. William Collins started as a Candleriggs-based printer/publisher in 1819, diversifying into reference and educational works, fiction and diaries. The rapidly expanding company moved to 144 Cathedral Street and became one of the world's foremost publishers. In 1989 the company merged with Harper & Row to become the publishing giant HarperCollins, and a few years later the stationery and diaries division hived off into Collins Debden, whose HQ is still at Bishopbriggs.

NEWSPAPERS

In 1657 the magistrates of Glasgow arranged for a copy of a 'diurnal' (i.e. a newspaper) to be occasionally sent to them from London. Prior to this very few people in Scotland – outside perhaps a few well-connected individuals in Edinburgh – would ever have seen a newspaper.

Before this date John Nicoll, a legal agent in Edinburgh, supplied the Glasgow magistrates with handwritten notes of 'weekly intelligence', that is, what we now call 'news'.

Glasgow's first home-grown newspaper was the *Courant* (afterwards called the *West Country Intelligence*), launched in 1715. It cost one penny and was published three times a week, exclusively available from the college printing-house or the post office. It did not last long.

A DULL DAY FOR OUR EDITORS.

In 1741 the *Glasgow Journal* was launched. It somehow failed to report the most momentous news of the time, the entry into the city of Bonnie Prince Charlie's army during the Jacobite Rebellion of 1745–6.

In 1804 the *Glasgow Advertiser*, also known as the *Herald and Advertiser and Commercial Chronicle*, was transformed into the *Glasgow Herald*, still the city's leading daily paper (known just as the *Herald* since 1992). In its early decades the *Glasgow Herald* was published three times a week, only becoming a daily in 1859.

The first Glasgow daily paper was actually the *Day*, which lasted for just six months in 1832.

Editorially, Glasgow's many newspapers in the nineteenth century supported a range of political positions. The *Free Press*, *Scots Times* and the *Argus* were Liberal, the *Chronicle* was Whig, while the leaning of the *Tory Courier* was obvious. For thirty-four years from 1831 the *Loyal Reformer's Gazette* fought for political reform, its editor Peter Mackenzie being jailed under the repressive Gagging Acts.

These days Glasgow is the HQ for not just the *Herald*, but also the *Daily Record*, the *Evening Times*, the *Scottish Sun*, the *Scottish Mirror*, the *Scottish Daily Express*, the *Scottish Daily Mail*, the *Sunday Mail*, the *Sunday Post*, the *Scottish News of the World* and the *Sunday Times Scotland*, as well as BBC Scotland and STV. Edinburgh may be the capital and have the parliament, but Glasgow is Scotland's media centre.

LIBRARIES

The Mitchell Library is the largest reference library in Europe, holding more than 1,213,000 books and over 15,000 periodical titles. It is one of the depository libraries of Britain and an institution of recognised international significance. The distinctive copper dome, topped by the female statue of Literature, is a common landmark

from the M8. The main building opened in 1911, and was extended in the 1970s after the adjacent St Andrew's Halls burned down.

The façade of St Andrew's Halls can still be seen on Granville Street, with Titans and Caryatids supporting groups of statues, including Homer, Shakespeare, Michelangelo, Leonardo da Vinci, and Greek gods.

Many of the most consulted books are in the Glasgow Room, which also holds more than 2,000 volumes of local newspapers and thousands of photographs. The library has put many of its local holdings online as part of the Virtual Mitchell project.

The Mitchell also has a lending library section. There are 33 other lending libraries in the City of Glasgow. The Maryhill building is one of the original Carnegie libraries, one of the many such institutions built with money donated by the businessman and philanthropist Andrew Carnegie (1835–1919). Another lending library is beneath the Gallery of Modern Art (GoMA) on Queen Street.

TWELVE WELL-KNOWN GLASGOW MUSEUMS

Glasgow has almost twice as many museums as Edinburgh.

1. The **Kelvingrove Museum and Art Gallery** is claimed to be the most visited free-to-enter visitor attraction in Scotland as well as the most popular UK museum outside London. The building is beautifully decorated with numerous statues and carvings – including some hidden behind the topmost towers that cannot be seen by anyone except birds and the occasional maintenance worker.

2. Wealthy industrialist Sir William Burrell was a magpie-type collector of fine objects, and the **Burrell Collection** is a 9,000-exhibit testament to his eclectic taste, mixing archaeological and medieval items with paintings, carpets and the decorative arts. When Burrell deeded the collection to Glasgow in 1944 he specified it should be on view at least 16 miles from Glasgow, so as to avoid urban hideousness and air pollution. After years of fruitless searching the trustees waived this part of the requirement when Pollok Estate was gifted to the city. Although Pollok was only a few miles from the centre, its bucolic 360 acres proved a perfect embodiment of Burrell's desire for a beautiful home for his beautiful objects. The purpose-built building opened in 1983.

3. The Cedar Room in **Pollok House** may be where a group of concerned conservationists met to create the National Trust for Scotland. Elsewhere among the mansion's exhibits can be found several large oil paintings of the Spanish Habsburg royal family; look closely and you can see the malformed facial features, brought about by several generations of inbreeding.

4. The largest object in a local museum is a Glasgow-built South African locomotive, located in the new **Riverside Museum (the Museum of Transport)** in Yorkhill. The museum, which opened in 2011 on the site of the former A. & J. Inglis shipyard (where the paddle steamer *Waverley* was built) stands alongside the tall ship *Glenlee*, one of only five Clyde-built sailing ships still afloat.

5. The **Gallery of Modern Art** (GoMA) on Queen Street is the most visited contemporary art gallery in Scotland.

6. The **St Mungo Museum of Religious Life and Art,** close to the cathedral, is home to not only a spectacular set of items relating to the many forms of religious belief, but also the first Zen garden in the UK.

7. Opposite the St Mungo Museum is **Provand's Lordship,** one of the oldest houses in Glasgow, built in 1471. It once belonged to a canon of the cathedral when this area was at the very heart of the tiny village of Glasgow.

8. The **Hunterian Museum** in the University of Glasgow is an absorbing collection of archaeology, ethnographic objects, fossils, the history of science and natural history. Highlights include the world's smallest dinosaur footprint, specimens of extinct animals such as the dodo, blue antelope and thylacine, and a wall-sized map of the earth, made in China in 1674.

9. The **Hunterian Art Gallery** opposite has a recreation of a Charles Rennie Mackintosh interior.

10. The **People's Palace** houses a wealth of evocative items illustrating Glasgow's social history, including recreations of a single-room tenement family flat from the 1930s and a Barlinnie jail cell.

11. The **Glasgow Science Centre** on Pacific Quay is stuffed full of interactive hands-on exhibits, not to mention live critters such as Giant African Land Snails and Madagascan Hissing Cockroaches.

12. The **Scottish Football Museum** at Hampden lays claim to 'the world's most impressive national collection of football related objects, memorabilia and ephemera' and was the first football museum in the world. Its exhibits include the Scottish Cup, the oldest football trophy in the world.

TWELVE LESS WELL-KNOWN GLASGOW MUSEUMS

1. The **Scotland Street Museum,** in a former school designed by Charles Rennie Mackintosh, tells the story of education in Scotland – complete with reconstructed classrooms.

2. Tucked into an industrial estate in Nitshill is the **Glasgow Museums Resource Centre (GMRC),** where a million objects are stored because there is no room to display them in the city's principal museums. This cavernous treasure trove of wonders can be visited, for free, on pre-arranged guided tours.

3. Thousands of people stream past it every day, but few notice the **Royal Highland Fusiliers Museum** on Sauchiehall Street. Beginning in 1678, it tells the story of the Royal Scots Fusiliers, the Highland Light Infantry and the City of Glasgow Regiment, and also houses exhibits on the 602 City of Glasgow Squadron.

4. Want to know more about the Highland Bagpipe? The **Museum of Piping**, an offshoot of Edinburgh's National Museum of Scotland, can be found in National Piping Centre on Hope Street.

5. The best 'unknown museum' is the **Zoology Museum**, hidden within the labyrinth of the University of Glasgow. Once located, it is a wonderland of animal skeletons – everything from an anaconda to a vampire bat – along with weird insects, models of giant squid, and live creatures such as bearded dragons and tropical spiders.

6. Victoria Park shelters **Fossil Grove**, a covered-over setting of fossilised tree stumps, more than 330 million years old.

7. **Springburn Museum** is very much a community enterprise, drawing on evocative objects and photographs that tell the social, industrial and political experiences of local people, especially from the railway era.

8. The **Tenement House** on Buccleuch Street is not a restoration but an actual time machine into the past, the 'preserved-in-amber' quality coming from the fact that the last tenant lived there for more than 50 years – and never threw anything away! For visitors of a certain age, the smell of the gas lighting will be an instant return to earlier times.

9. **Holmwood House** in Cathcart is a domestic villa designed by Alexander 'Greek' Thomson. It remains open while being conserved by the National Trust for Scotland, so that the long-term conservation process can be seen in action.

10. **Provan Hall** near Easterhouse may be older than Provand's Lordship, possibly dating to the 1450s. Its twin buildings set around a courtyard wonderfully evoke what would have been a medieval 'country house' or hunting lodge.

11. **Glasgow Police Museum** on Bell Street tells the story of the City of Glasgow Police from 1779 to 1975, as well as displaying police uniforms and insignia from all over the world.

12. Easily the least-visited museum is the **Anatomy Museum** within the university, which can only be accessed by special appointment. It is used for teaching and research for medical and veterinary students, and mostly consists of preserved specimens of human and animal body parts.

MUSEUM CURIOSITIES

Among the tens of thousands of genuine items at Kelvingrove is a composite fake creature created by museum staff out of fish and animal parts, and labelled *Haggis scoticus* (Scottish Haggis).

One of Kelvingrove's treasures is Salvador Dali's painting 'Christ of St John of the Cross'. The unorthodox religious aspect of the painting has meant it has been attacked twice – first by a man employing a sharp stone and then his bare hands, and secondly by an individual wielding an airgun, the bullet bouncing off the new protecting transparent cover.

Kelvingrove returned a bloodstained shirt from the Ghost Dance period to its Native American custodians in 1999. The shirt was reportedly removed in 1890 from the body of a Lakota warrior after the massacre of Wounded Knee. This was the first such repatriation from outside America.

Auguste Rodin's 'Age of Bronze', a sculpture of a handsome naked youth, once stood on display at Kelvingrove. So many female visitors stroked the statue's genitals that the bronze patina wore off. The bronze has now been restored, and the sculpture stands unmolested in the Burrell Collection.

The Hunterian started with a diverse collection assembled by the pioneering Scottish anatomist and scientist William Hunter. One of the anatomical curiosities is labelled as 'A Honeymooner's Heart'. This belonged to an old man who had married his much younger maid, and then died suddenly during his wedding night.

In 2001 a full-size Tyrannosaurus Rex was installed outside the Hunterian to publicise a 'Walking with Dinosaurs' exhibition. The T Rex rapidly became a local landmark, and lasted long after the exhibition closed, finally becoming extinct in 2005.

It is common to find statues representing art or philosophy on museums – but on the façade of the People's Palace there are female personifications of the things that made Glasgow great: Shipbuilding, Mathematics, Engineering and Textile Manufacture.

ART

Robert Foulis, printer to the University of Glasgow, opened the first school for painting and sculpture in about 1750.

The Glasgow School of Art has an international reputation for turning out notable practitioners in all areas of the arts. Famous alumni include photographers Harry Benson and Oscar Marzaroli, artists David Shrigley, Jenny Saville, Jim Lambie and Ken Currie, illustrator Jessie Marion King, poet Ian Hamilton Finlay, filmmakers Norman McLaren and Alexander Mackendrick, playwrights Liz Lochhead and John Byrne, and actors Peter Capaldi and Robbie Coltrane. Robbie Coltrane returned to the school to film *Tutti Frutti*, the 1987 television series scripted by John Byrne.

In 2009 and 2010 two Glaswegian artists in succession won the Turner Prize. Richard Wright received the 2009 award for a golden fresco exhibited on the walls of Tate Britain, while the following year Susan Philipsz from Maryhill became the first sound installation artist to win the prize. Her piece, originally commissioned by the Glasgow International Festival, involved an ethereal *a cappella* rendering of the traditional lament 'Lowlands Away' – the tale of a woman visited by the ghost of her sailor lover – played over a public address system from beneath the George V Bridge, the Caledonian Railway Bridge and Glasgow Bridge.

The Turner had previously been awarded to Glasgow artists Douglas Gordon (1996) and Martin Creed (2001), the latter winning for exhibiting a light switching on and off in an empty room, which prompted controversy about the relevance and meaning of modern art.

The floor of the People's Palace features murals painted by Ken Currie in 1987, depicting working class and trade union struggle, including the massacre of the Calton Weavers.

Leading novelist Alasdair Gray's mural and ceiling paintings can be seen in the Oran Mor pub and Ubiquitous Chip bar in the West End.

In 1987 eight male statues at the Glasgow School of Art had their pudenda removed by an unknown critic.

CHARLES RENNIE MACKINTOSH

The Glasgow School of Art was designed by the celebrated Art Nouveau architect and artist Charles Rennie Mackintosh (1868–1928). Ray McKenzie's *Sculpture in Glasgow* describes the style of the Renfield Street building as 'pure "Spook School"'.

More Mackintosh buildings and designs can be admired at Scotland Street School Museum, the Willow Tea Rooms on Sauchiehall Street, the Lighthouse on Mitchell Lane, Martyrs' School on Parson Street in Townhead (close to where Mackintosh was born), Ruchill Church Hall on Shakespeare Street, and the former Daily Record building on Renfield Lane.

One structure which Mackintosh did not build himself is the House for An Art Lover, in Bellahouston Park; it was completed in 1996 using designs CRM had submitted for a competition in a German magazine in 1901.

Many of Mackintosh's designs were achieved in collaboration with his wife, Margaret MacDonald.

There are permanent Mackintosh exhibitions in the Kelvingrove Art Gallery and Museum and the Hunterian Art Gallery. Along with Brussels, Paris, Barcelona, Prague and Helsinki, Glasgow is on the circuit for aficionados of European Art Nouveau.

The interior Mackintosh designed for Househill Mansion was lost when the grand house burned down in the 1930s.

The Charles Rennie Mackintosh Society is based in another of his buildings, the former Queen's Cross Church at the junction of Garscube Road and Maryhill Road in Maryhill. A Mackintosh trail leaflet is available.

SONGS ABOUT GLASGOW

The quintessential Glasgow song is 'I Belong To Glasgow', written and performed by the music hall entertainer Will Fyffe (who was

from Dundee). According to one story, Fyffe met an intoxicated individual at Glasgow Central station, and asked him, 'Do you belong to Glasgow?' The man genially replied, 'At the moment, Glasgow belongs to me.' Everyone knows the rousing chorus, but fewer make it to the final line, in which the drunk makes it home and states, 'You don't give a hang [damn] for the wife.' Glasgow's Empire Theatre ran a Will Fyffe competition, where each contestant had to perform a version of 'I Belong To Glasgow'. Fyffe himself entered in disguise; he came second.

The vast majority of popular songs concerning Glasgow are sectarian in nature, unpleasantly valorising one religion or cultural identity, or denigrating the 'opposing side'.

Recent folk songs about the city include the nostalgic 'Oh where is the Glasgow' by Adam McNaughton (who also wrote children's favourite 'The Jeely Piece Song', about jelly sandwiches), and the resolutely anti-sentimental 'Farewell to Glasgow' written by Jim McLean, which enumerates the horrors of tenement living. Another folk favourite, Harry Hagan's 'Sam The Skull', is the eponymous tale of a tough streetwise Glasgow cat.

ABBA's mega-hit 'Super Trouper' is told from the point of view of a disenchanted touring musician staying in a hotel in Glasgow.

The name of the American group A Sunny Day in Glasgow is a sarcastic reference to the city's weather patterns.

The title of Deacon Blue's debut album *Raintown* is another direct reference to the less-than-sunny climate of a certain West of Scotland metropolis. The band's song 'Christmas and Glasgow' is about a couple working out their relationship over the seasonal holidays in Glasgow.

Eddi Reader's 'Glasgow Star' celebrates a successful day busking in Buchanan Street.

Franz Ferdinand's single 'Do You Want To' mentions Glasgow art gallery Transmission, noted for its trendy parties.

Billy Connolly has recorded several songs about his home city, from the nostalgic – 'I Wish I Was In Glasgow' – to the humorous – 'Last Train Tae Glasgow Central', which describes fare-dodging on a train back from a holiday.

'Sealed With A Glasgow Kiss' by Carter The Unstoppable Sex Machine is a grim tale of a relationship degenerating into domestic violence – a 'Glasgow Kiss' is a head-butt.

The Glasgow comedy band Hugh Reed & The Velvet Underpants were noted for song titles such as 'Take a Walk on the Clydeside', a pun on the Lou Reed hit 'Walk on the Wild Side'.

The Mogwai track 'Glasgow Mega-Snake' is a thundering prog-rock instrumental.

Hue and Cry's celebratory 'Mother Glasgow' mentions the symbols on the Glasgow coat of arms – the tree, the fish, the bird and the bell – and finishes with the motto, 'Let Glasgow Flourish!'

TOP ROCKERS

In 2003 the *Scotsman* polled over 50 musicians and critics to find the Top 100 Scottish albums. At number one was *Screamadelica* by Glasgow band Primal Scream. Other denizens of the greater Glasgow area in the top ten were The Average White Band, The Blue Nile, John Martyn, The Jesus and Mary Chain, Bert Jansch and Teenage Fanclub.

Bellshill's Teenage Fanclub had four albums in the Top 100, more than any other artist.

Other artists with Glasgow-area connections in the Top 100 included Altered Images, Aztec Camera, The Bathers, Belle and Sebastian, The Bluebells, Lloyd Cole and the Commotions, Edwyn Collins, Deacon Blue, Del Amitri, The Delgados, Hipsway, Love and Money, Frankie Miller, Mogwai, Orange Juice, The Pastels, Gerry Rafferty, Stone The Crows, Texas, Travis and The Vaselines.

Also on the list were 1970s group Blue. In 2003 they failed in a court case to prevent the boy band Blue from using the name.

IT'S ONLY ROCK 'N' ROLL BUT WE LIKE IT

Glasgow-born Lonnie Donegan invented the musical style known as skiffle, mixing folk, blues, country and rock 'n' roll, thus paving the way for 'beat' music and changing popular music forever.

Creation Records boss Alan McGee, who grew up in Glasgow, started his record label in 1983 with a £1,000 loan, releasing a single by Glasgow obscurities The Legend. In 1993 he signed Oasis after seeing them play a gig at a tiny Glasgow venue, King Tut's Wah Wah Hut. Oasis have currently sold in excess of 50 million records and McGee has had an immense impact on popular music as a record label owner, band manager and entrepreneur.

Tigermilk, the first album by Belle and Sebastian, was recorded at Stow College in 1996 as part of the music course attended by the group. Under the terms of the course, just 1,000 copies were pressed. The album was given a larger release several years later when the band had achieved mainstream success.

Glasgow hi-fi manufacturer Linn Electronics sponsored the first recording of The Blue Nile, as a way of showcasing the company's very high-quality audio systems. In 1983 Linn created their own record label to release the band's debut album, *A Walk Across The Rooftops*.

Brian Robertson from Clarkston was one of the twin lead guitarists who gave the distinctive double harmony guitar sound to 1970s rockers Thin Lizzy. He later played with heavy metal bands Wild Horses and Motorhead.

Cream, the 1960s power trio/supergroup who had hits with 'Sunshine of Your Love', 'White Room' and 'I Feel Free', featured Eric Clapton on guitar, Ginger Baker on drums, and, on bass, Glaswegian Jack Bruce. Their *Wheels Of Fire* LP became the first album to go platinum. Bruce went on to have a successful solo career and is often thought as being one of the greatest bass players in the world.

Singer Frankie Miller from Bridgeton, whose hits 'Darlin'' and 'Caledonia' remain perennial favourites, suffered a brain haemorrhage in 1994. Despite spending five months in a coma, he continues to record today.

In 2005 indie songwriter Edwyn Collins, whose million-selling hit 'A Girl Like You' is one of the classic love songs of its time, collapsed with a brain haemorrhage. After recovering from a coma and undergoing extensive therapy to combat dysphasia, he returned to performing.

Midge Ure of Slik and Ultravox was one of the prime movers behind Band Aid.

In 1965 The Beatstalkers, performing a free show in George Square, were overwhelmed by the crowd numbers and two of the band had to escape to the City Chambers on the back of police horses.

In 2004–5 Franz Ferdinand won the Mercury Music Prize, an Ivor Novello Award, and two awards at the BRITS, for Best British Group and Best British Rock Act. Although alluding to the Austrian aristocrat whose assassination led to the First World War, the band's name was originally inspired by a racehorse named Archduke Ferdinand.

Glasgow has long had a thriving 'underground' or 'alternative' scene, with critical (and sometimes commercial) success being achieved by the likes of Aereogramme, Bis, Camera Obscura, The Delgados, The Fast Camels, The Fratellis, Glasvegas, Mogwai and The Phantom Band.

Glasgow has been the base of many influential independent record labels, including Postcard Records, Rock Action Records, Neon Tetra Records and Chemikal Underground.

In 2007 Chemikal Underground released *Ballads of the Book*, a collaboration between contemporary Scottish rock musicians and authors, partly funded by the Scottish Arts Council. Among the poets involved was Edwin Morgan, while the novelists included A.L. Kennedy, Alasdair Gray and Louise Welsh.

Ricky Gardiner of 1970s Glasgow prog-rockers Beggars Opera co-wrote one of the most covered of alternative rock songs, Iggy Pop's 'The Passenger'.

During an otherwise sunny Glastonbury festival in 1999, it started to rain during Travis's set. Their hit single at the time was called 'Why Does It Always Rain On Me?'

BEFORE (AND AFTER) THEY WERE FAMOUS

Eddi Reader, originally from Anderston, and who later had an enduring hit with the Fairground Attraction folk-rock song 'Perfect', performed her first professional gig as backing singer with the agit prop punk group The Gang of Four.

Simple Minds, the Glasgow stadium rock group *par excellence*, started life as the punk group Johnny & The Self-Abusers, who split up on the same day as they released their one and only single.

Alan Mair of The Beatstalkers ended up running a stall in Kensington Market making leather boots. On one occasion he gave a free pair to a down-on-his-luck David Bowie – the fitting was performed by Mair's young assistant, an aspiring singer named Freddie Mercury.

Sushil K. Dade of The Soup Dragons/Future Pilot AKA is now a driving instructor and has taught members of The Pastels and Teenage Fanclub.

THE SENSATIONAL ALEX HARVEY

Alex Harvey (1935–82) is often considered as Glasgow's greatest rock star. He had slogged his way through the worlds of skiffle, jazz, folk, rock 'n' roll, blues, soul, R 'n' B, psychedelia and musical theatre before achieving success with the Sensational Alex Harvey Band, when he was almost in his forties.

He first came to prominence in 1957 when he won a talent contest organised by the *Sunday Mail,* who were looking for 'Scotland's answer to Tommy Steele'. Harvey performed a wild version of 'Hound Dog' on a cheap pre-war Gibson guitar he had rebuilt himself. One of the other finalists was Sydney Devine, later Scotland's multi-million selling 'Rhinestone Cowboy'.

Before his status as a teen idol, Tommy Steele had been a merchant seaman. When the two met, Harvey broke into Glasgow docks so that Steele could meet his former shipmates. The pair of nascent pop stars were discovered and had to scarper.

After the talent contest Harvey was in such demand he cloned himself – on any given Saturday night there might be up to five Alex Harveys playing across Scotland, all of them mates of the original. The Alex Harvey Soul Band later toured the Outer Hebrides pretending to be Johnny and the Hurricanes, who had just had a hit with 'Red River Rock' and so were thought to be a bigger draw.

For five years from 1966 Harvey was in the house band of the London-based musical *Hair,* notorious for its nudity and hippie-era politics.

In 1975 the Sensational Alex Harvey Band (SAHB) were the biggest-grossing live act in the UK, delighting audiences with a mixture of heavy rock, theatricality and silly dances. Chris Glen of SAHB was voted the wearer of the third-best codpiece in rock, after Larry Blackmon of Cameo and Ian Anderson of Jethro Tull. Glen maintained that his codpiece protected sensitive parts from his heavy bass guitar.

One of SAHB's live showstoppers was 'Framed', a tale of a man 'set up' by the police. At their triumphant Christmas shows at the Glasgow Apollo in 1975, Harvey asked the rhetorical question, 'Do you believe me?' – and an audience member shouted out, 'Naw! You shagged my sister in 1971.' Harvey took to playing 'Framed' dressed as Hitler (while also lecturing the audience on the dangers of Fascism), while for his last show with SAHB, at the Reading Festival in 1977, he came on dressed as Jesus, in a loincloth and a crown of thorns made of real barbed wire, which caused him to bleed profusely. The large polystyrene cross he was carrying was 'accidentally' dropped on the DJ Alan 'Fluff' Freeman.

After he left SAHB, Harvey's albums included *The Mafia Stole My Guitar,* named after a real incident in America when the band's equipment was stolen by The Mob.

Harvey had an abiding interest in the supernatural. He believed he had been a Highland soldier in a previous life, fighting at the Battle of Waterloo. *Alex Harvey Presents: The Loch Ness Monster* came out in 1977, a spoken-word album consisting of interviews with people around Loch Ness who claimed to have seen the creature, with narration by Richard O'Brien of *Rocky Horror Picture Show* fame. Harvey had previously written a song about Nessie,

'The Water Beastie', for the album *Rock Drill*, while a track on the album *Framed* told the story of Isobel Goudie, who had been burned as a witch in Auldearn in 1662.

Harvey, like his father and his grandfather before him, was a registered conscientious objector.

POP ON THE SCREEN

Clare Grogan of Glasgow group Altered Images appeared as Gregory's unexpected girlfriend in the film *Gregory's Girl* and as Lister's unrequited love interest Kristine Z. Kochanski in the first two series of cult comedy television series *Red Dwarf*.

In 1980 Glaswegian Sheena Easton, who had come to fame via *The Big Time*, a television 'reality' documentary about a pop hopeful, had two songs in the top ten at the same time – '9 to 5' and 'Modern Girl'. A year later she recorded the title tune for the James Bond film *For Your Eyes Only*.

The Trashcan Sinatras promoted their album *A Happy Pocket* with a 15-minute *film noir* named *Spooktime*, filmed at various seedy venues around Glasgow, including the George Hotel on Buchanan Street.

Fans of *The Sopranos* TV series will be familiar with the show's title track, 'Woke Up This Morning' by Alabama 3. Despite their name the group is British and their vocalist, The Very Reverend Dr D. Wayne Love, grew up as plain Jake Black in Glasgow.

'Stuck In The Middle With You' by Stealers Wheel – the duo formed by Glaswegians Gerry Rafferty and Joe Egan – was famously used in the Quentin Tarantino film *Reservoir Dogs,* the track's gently melodic soft rock contrasting with the on-screen violence.

Glasgow's musical nightlife was the backdrop for *Living Apart Together* (1983), the tale of a rock singer (played by real-life pop star B.A. Robertson) trying to sort out his personal problems.

The 1949 film *Floodtide* featured the Barrowlands Ballroom resident band, Billy MacGregor and the Gaybirds.

'Don't You (Forget About Me)' featured on the soundtrack of teen movie *The Breakfast Club,* giving Simple Minds a number one hit in America.

SOME GLASGOW NUMBER ONES

The first Glaswegian number one – indeed the first chart-topper by a Scottish band – was achieved by The Marmalade in 1969, with their cover of The Beatles' 'Ob-La-Di, Ob-La-Da'. For their triumphal appearance on *Top of the Pops* they dressed in kilts. The band had a second number one the same year with 'Reflections Of My Life'.

In 1975 The Average White Band reached number one in the USA with 'Pick Up the Pieces'. The same year Billy Connolly topped the UK charts with his parody of a Tammy Wynette song, 'D.I.V.O.R.C.E.'.

Kelly Marie (real name Jacqueline McKinnon, from Paisley), had a number one in 1980 with the disco song 'Feels Like I'm In Love'.

'Don't Leave Me This Way' (number one for The Communards in 1986) featured the distinctive vocals of Glaswegian singer Jimmy Somerville. As a solo artist, Somerville scored a number one hit in the US dance chart with 'Heartbeat' in 1995.

In 1988 'Perfect' by Fairground Attraction was followed to the UK number one slot by Wet Wet Wet's 'With A Little Help From My Friends'.

Simple Minds achieved their first UK number one in 1989 with 'Belfast Child'. The same year Texas topped the singles charts with 'I Don't Want A Lover', while Deacon Blue had a number one album with *When The Whole World Knows Your Name*.

Wet Wet Wet's 'Love Is All Around', taken from the film *Four Weddings and A Funeral*, hogged the number one spot for fifteen weeks in 1994.

MUSICIANS BORN IN GLASGOW
WHO MOVED AWAY WHEN YOUNG

Lonnie Donegan (born in Bridgeton, raised in London).

Folk guitar master Bert Jansch (brought up in Edinburgh).

Mark Knopfler of Dire Straits (moved to Northumberland aged seven).

Flower power icon Donovan (born in Maryhill, moved to Hertfordshire at the age of nine).

Folk-rocker Al Stewart (born in Glasgow, raised in Dorset).

Schoolboy-attired Angus Young, along with his brother Malcolm, both Glaswegian-born guitarists with rock titans AC/DC, was brought up in Australia.

COMEDIANS

Following an especially witty heckle during one of his shows, English comic John Hegarty quipped that it was well known that in Glasgow, the audience were often funnier than the act they had come to see. In a city of natural comedians, however, the big banana is without doubt Billy Connolly. From his early days poking fun at religious shibboleths to his groundbreaking appearances on the *Parkinson* show and his multiple series of *Billy Connolly's World Tour of . . .* , he has been at the forefront of taboo-breaking laugh-making. And in a culture where bigotry and ignorance can at times seem all too prevalent, the Big Yin is a true voice of reason and liberty.

8

SPORTS & GAMES

Glasgow is irretrievably linked with football, but there is much more to the Glaswegian passion for sport than Celtic v Rangers, something that will become clear in 2014 when the city hosts the Commonwealth Games. And in recent years it has been chosen for the UEFA Champions League final (2002), the Special Olympics (2005), the UEFA Cup final (2007), the World Acrobatic Gymnastic Championships (2008) and the Commonwealth Table Tennis Championships (2009).

Sport wasn't always officially approved. In 1589 the Kirk Session banned football, golf and shinty from being played in churchyards.

Twenty-seven sports-related buildings in Glasgow are listed for their local, national or international architectural or historical significance.

ATHLETICS AND RUNNING

Eric Liddell, famously depicted in the film *Chariots of Fire*, made his final track appearance in Glasgow in 1925, just before becoming a missionary in China. He was participating in the annual Scottish Amateur Athletics Association championship at Hampden Park.

Several football clubs, including Celtic, Rangers and Queen's Park, held athletics events to bring in income during the summer season. The competitions were especially popular in the 1920s and '30s, and continued at Ibrox into the early 1960s.

Former Liberal Democrat leader Menzies 'Ming' Campbell broke the British 100m sprint record when he was a student at the University of Glasgow in 1964.

In 2009 the Great Scottish Run, which finishes at Glasgow Green, had 21,000 participants.

The Scotstoun Stadium, opened in 2010, is now Scotland's leading athletics venue. The new Sir Chris Hoy Velodrome and National Indoor Sports Arena, based in the East End, will open for the Commonwealth Games.

BOWLS

The rules of modern bowling were formulated in Glasgow in 1848.

Local firm Thomas Taylor is the world's oldest manufacturer of bowls and bowls equipment. They have a small historical exhibition at their premises on Bernard Street. The firm started making bowls in 1796 – alongside artificial limbs for men wounded in the Napoleonic Wars.

There are only eleven places in the world where bowls are tested before being stamped with an identifying letter. All bowls marked with an 'A' come from Glasgow.

The city has the highest concentration of bowling greens anywhere in the UK, with 87 clubs, of which 12 are over 150 years old.

Wellcroft Bowling Club, founded in 1835, is one of three clubs that lays claim to being the oldest in the city.

The playing of bowls in Glasgow dates to at least 1595.

In 2006 Balornock Bowling Club's new clubhouse was one of two buildings in Scotland to win a Civic Trust Award for design. The other was the Scottish Parliament.

BOXING

Formal boxing bouts have typically taken place in football stadia. In 1980 local man Jim Watt beat Howard Davis in a lightweight contest at Ibrox, watched by 20,000 fans singing 'Flower of Scotland'. In a 2000 match at Hampden Park, Mike Tyson KO'd Lou Savarese after just 38 seconds. The same venue saw Scottish flyweight Jackie Paterson fight in six fights during the 1940s.

Glasgow's most celebrated boxer was world flyweight champion Benny Lynch, who was greeted by a crowd of 100,000 when he returned from winning the title at Wembley Stadium. He died of alcoholism and malnutrition in 1946 at the age of thirty-three. Benny Lynch Court stands near his birthplace of Florence Street in Gorbals, and his restored grave at St Kentigern's Cemetery now reads, 'Undefeated Flyweight Champion of the World, the first Scotsman to win a world boxing title. Erected by boxing fans'.

DARTS

Darts was banned in Glasgow pubs in the 1930s, in an attempt to limit the consumption of alcohol.

CRICKET

Cricket has been played in Glasgow since at least 1826, and the oldest still existing club, Clydesdale CC, was founded in 1848. Despite its genteel image, the sport was popular with aggressively competitive working-class players.

In 1894 a ball struck from the Titwood ground in Pollokshields landed on a moving goods train on the adjacent rail line. It was recovered at Carlisle.

CURLING AND ICE SPORTS

There were once almost 100 outdoor curling ponds in the city, their popularity boosted by a series of exceptionally cold winters during the nineteenth century.

In 1842 'Long' John Anderson, a member of the Partick club, played non-stop for 36 hours, often by candlelight. He was still curling at the age of eighty-six.

In 1896 a temporary indoor ice rink was set up in an entertainment venue on Sauchiehall Street. A more satisfactory affair – indeed, the first purpose-built ice rink in Scotland – was erected at Crossmyloof in 1907. Barring a few years following its use as an aero engine factory in the First World War, the rink was used for competitions until 1986. The area's sole competitive ice rink is now the Braehead Arena in Renfrew.

FOOTBALL

Ball games in Glasgow in one form or another go back to the 1570s, when a 'ba' game' was played on Shrove Tuesday, with balls supplied by the town council. It was a roughhouse, in which two mob-like groups attempted to get 'their' ball past a destination in the street – by any means necessary.

By the early nineteenth century teams with fixed numbers and goalposts were established in Glasgow, although the game still had a long way to go. In the later part of the century Queen's Park FC were playing what they called the 'passing game', in which individual players, instead of keeping the ball to themselves, passed it to team-members if they had a better chance of scoring a goal. Out of these games developed the rules of modern-day Association Football.

The first ever international football game in the world took place on 20 November 1872, at Hamilton Crescent Cricket Ground in Partick, home of the West of Scotland Cricket Club. The result was England 0–0 Scotland, and the entire Scotland team were drawn from the ranks of Queen's Park, Glasgow's premier football club.

The Scottish Cup, awarded to the winners of a knockout competition, was instigated in 1873. It is the oldest Association Football trophy in the world.

Football in Glasgow flourished quickly and fiercely. Rangers was founded in 1873, Celtic in 1887. Both were religiously partisan from the beginning, leading to a sectarian divide that has blighted Scottish football ever since, especially since the 'Old Firm' dominate the Scottish Premier League and the Scottish Cup. The Scottish Football League was formed in 1890. Its members that decade included Clyde FC, Linthouse FC, Third Lanark FC and Partick Thistle FC. The first named moved to Cumbernauld in 1994, the second no longer exist, and the third are now an amateur team, but First Division Partick Thistle are Glasgow's third most successful club – although they are not based in Partick any more.

MORE FOOTBALL RESULTS.

Jock. "Th' Sco'sh ha' woon, lassie."   *Jean.* "*So I see!*"

Queen's Park operated out of Hampden Park, whose 'historic sporting cluster' now contains the oldest buildings in the world that are still used for football. The changing rooms and groundsman's shed at Lesser Hampden off Cathcart Road date from before 1850, as they used to form part of Clincart Farm, on whose fields the football pitch was laid out.

As gate numbers and income increased, rivalry broke out between the major clubs in the building of stadia that could not only accommodate the weekly league games, but also major events such as cup finals and international matches. By the early twentieth century Glasgow had the three largest football stadia in the world – Celtic Park, Ibrox and Hampden Park.

The result of the 'stadium race' left Hampden Park with a capacity of 120,000 in 1910, so by default it became the standard venue for all major games. Upgraded to a 149,000 capacity in the 1930s, Hampden was unrivalled in the world until a larger stadium was built in Brazil in 1950. In 1970, 136,505 people watched Celtic v Leeds in a European Cup semi-final, while three years later 127,714 fans cheered on Rangers and Celtic in the Scottish Cup final. However, this was the last time a six-figure crowd attended. Safety issues and major changes in stadium design – partly brought about by the Hillsborough disaster in 1989 – saw capacities restricted. Hampden was completely rebuilt and the venue can now take a maximum of 52,000 fans for internationals and cup finals. Queen's Park are now in the Third Division of the Scottish League, and their average attendance at the vast stadium is only in the hundreds.

Hampden was one of the projects of Glasgow-based engineer Archibald Leitch, the world's first specialist stadium designer. His clients included Manchester United, Arsenal, Chelsea, Fulham, Tottenham Hotspur, Aston Villa, Everton, Liverpool, Sheffield Wednesday, Sheffield United and clubs in Edinburgh and Dundee, as well as Rangers' Ibrox Stadium.

Much to the annoyance of an attacking team, the older Hampden Park had square goalposts, which caused the ball to bounce off them back onto the pitch instead of into the goal. The stadium hosts the Scottish Football Museum, and a pair of the square posts are on display there.

The first black footballer in Scottish, then English, and finally international football was Guyana-born Andrew Watson, who started his career with Queen's Park and captained the Scottish national team in 1881 before moving to London.

The world's first 'football special' train brought 1,000 Brummies to Glasgow in 1884, to see Queen's Park beat Aston Villa 6–1 in the English FA Cup final. Many of the fans missed their train back and slept out in the open around the pitch, cheered by medicinal quantities of alcohol.

Celtic's famous green-and-white hoops were only introduced in 1903, replacing a strip with vertical stripes in the same colours. Rangers, who had played in full royal blue since their inception, experimented with blue and white hoops in 1882, but a fan rebellion forced a reversion to the original strip.

In 2002 fans voted Jimmy 'Jinky' Johnstone as the greatest ever Celtic player. He was one of the 'Lisbon Lions' of 1967, the first British team to win the European Cup. A statue of the footballer now stands outside Celtic Park, close to a sculpture of Brother Walfrid, the priest who founded the club as a focus for Catholic Irish immigrants.

When referring to the football club, 'Celtic' is pronounced 'Seltic', and not 'Keltic', which is only used for the cultural identity.

Rangers' ground, Ibrox, has seen three different stadia since the previously peripatetic club settled there in 1887, and the first two were marked by tragedy. In 1892 a stand collapsed, killing two brothers. In 1902 part of the west terrace of the second stadium collapsed, causing twenty-six deaths and hundreds of injuries. There were two deaths in 1961 when a barrier collapsed, and more injuries in 1967 and 1969. Then on 2 January 1971, sixty-six people died and 145 were injured in Britain's worst football disaster, ushering in a new era of stadium design, seated stands, and limited numbers.

To give an example of how things have changed, Ibrox set the all-time UK league match record with an attendance of 118,567 in 1939, while in the 1970s Celtic Park was the largest club ground in the country. After vast expense and extensive redesigns, Ibrox Stadium's current maximum capacity is 50,411, while Celtic's average gate is about 57,000.

Toryglen Regional Football Centre, opened in 2009, has the first full-size indoor football pitch in Scotland.

FOX HUNTING

In 1907 the Lanarkshire and Renfrewshire Hunt overran the Cowglen Golf Club in Pollok Estate, causing £10 worth of damage. The toffs refused to pay.

GOLF

When most people think of golf in Scotland, they usually conjure up St Andrews. Yet, with fourteen public and four private courses, and sixty-six clubs, Glasgow has the greatest concentration of golf-related activity north of the border.

In 1577 students at the University of Glasgow were forbidden from indulging in billiards, dice or card games, but golf was acceptable, as long as it did not take place in churchyards.

The oldest club in the city is Glasgow Golf Club, which was founded on Glasgow Green in 1787. It is the ninth oldest club in the world. Among its heirlooms is the Silver Club, which records the winner of the annual tournament from 1787 to 1835 (with a gap between 1794 and 1809 during the Napoleonic Wars).

In 1949 eight out of ten players in the Ryder Cup were teeing off with clubs made by John Letters & Co. of Hillington, and Hollywood celebrities such as Danny Kaye, Bing Crosby and Bob Hope were endorsing the firm's products. Founded in 1918, the company dominated golf club manufacturing for decades, and is now a specialist brand. Meanwhile the St Mungo Manufacturing Company in Govan spent the 1930s turning out 10,000 golf balls a day.

Dr Alister MacKenzie, the 'Capability Brown of golf course design', reworked the course of Pollok Golf Club in 1922–24, charging a very reasonable £40 fee. The following decade, at the height of his worldwide fame, each commission was netting him thousands of pounds.

The very first Scottish Open was staged at the golf course of Haggs Castle, in 1986.

During the bad old days Glasgow's golf courses denied membership to Jews, so a group of Jewish golfers purchased their own course at Bonnyton in 1957.

HORSE RACING

The popular and occasionally riotous Pollokshaws Races were a fixture of working-class life from 1754 until 1841, the racecourse site now being occupied by Cowglen Golf Club. During the first year the ultimate winner of the many races received 20s prize money. Other, less pleasant, races took place in parallel, including cock races ('He that catches the cock in his teeth and walks three paces with him gets the cock and half a crown – their hands must be tied behind their backs') and goose races ('He that pulls off the head gets the goose').

ICE SKATING

The world's first guide for figure skaters appeared in 1852, authored by George Anderson, the President of Glasgow Skating Club.

QUOITS

Quoiting was once a serious rival to bowls, especially with coal miners, dockers and other 'work hard, play hard' Glaswegian men. The iron quoits themselves weighed between 10 and 16lb and had to be thrown towards a target some 18–21 yards away – this was one game that required both skill and muscles. The pursuit was taken very seriously at its clubs in Barrhead, Bridgeton, Dalmarnock and Pollokshaws, where heavy drinking and illegal gambling ensured the sport never achieved public respectability during its Victorian heyday.

RUGBY

Fixtures between the West of Scotland and Academicals rugby clubs were being held as early as 1867 (the Academicals were mostly students).

All rugby pitches in Britain have 'H'-shaped goalposts – except one. With special dispensation granted by the Scottish Rugby Union, Cartha Queen's Park RFC, who are based in Pollok Park, have goalposts shaped like tuning forks, with a single central support holding up the crossbar.

SHINTY

The Glasgow Celtic Society Cup dates from 1879, making it the oldest shinty trophy in the world. Shinty itself may be the most ancient game in Scotland, its true origins lost in the distant past, but possibly derived from the Irish colonisation of Western Scotland in the fourth and fifth centuries AD (it is related to the Irish sport of hurling). Being a team game played with curved sticks and a small solid ball, it bears a resemblance to both field hockey and ice hockey, sharing some of the tactics of the former and the physicality of the latter. The game remains a favourite with Highlanders, including those whose ancestors emigrated to the big cities.

SPORTS DAYS

During Glasgow's industrial heyday many large firms held an annual sports day. The Singer factory sports day was always highly regarded, and on one occasion in the 1950s the guest of honour was film star Dorothy Lamour.

SWIMMING AND BATHING

Swimming in the Clyde was popular because it was free, but male nakedness saw it banned in 1831, and by a few years later the sewage and industrial effluents effectively ended the pursuit.

Glasgow's first indoor subscription baths for the wealthy opened in 1804, near what is now Bath Street. The Arlington Baths Club, built in 1871 near St George's Cross, is the oldest surviving private swimming club in Britain, if not the world.

The bathsmaster at Arlington, William Wilson, wrote the first manuals on swimming, diving and life-saving, and also invented water polo (which he originally called aquatic football).

The world's first accredited ladies' swimming race took place at Townhead Baths in 1892. The winner, Miss E. Dobbie, swam the 200 yards in 4 minutes 25 seconds.

The city's first public baths were opened at Greenhead on the north side of Glasgow Green in 1880. Ten further municipal facilities were constructed, all soon becoming an integral part of working-class life. They offered a laundry, known as the 'steamie' to its exclusively female users, plus individual baths for personal washing, as well as a swimming pool. The pool and baths were emptied and refilled on Sundays, so the facilities were at their cheapest on Saturday nights when the water was dirtiest. The  North Woodside Baths in Braid Square, built in 1882, are now the oldest public baths that are still in use in the UK (although the water is now safe to use at all times!).

In the 1990s archaeologists looking for underground air raid shelters in Glasgow Green found the remains of an Olympic-sized open-air swimming pool. It had been filled in during the war before it was ever used, and so had been completely forgotten.

9

THE NATURAL WORLD

EARTHQUAKES

The earliest recorded earth tremor in Glasgow dates from 1570, when a short shaking caused the inhabitants 'to be in great terror and fear'.

More shocks were felt in 1608, 1650, 1656 and 1732, none of which seem to have caused much damage.

In 1754 a quake caused part of the riverside walk by Glasgow Green to collapse.

After more minor shocks in 1755, 1786, 1787, 1801, 1817, 1836, 1839, 1910 and 1978, the most intense event in the city for over two centuries occurred in December 1979, with a tremor registering 4.5 on the Richter Scale. There was another shock in July of 1984.

FOSSIL TREES

Fossil Grove in Victoria Park contains eleven *in situ* fossilised tree stumps from the Lower Carboniferous period – some 330 million years ago. There is also a section of a tree trunk.

Following its discovery in 1887, Fossil Grove was the first geological site in the world to be protected within a purpose-built building.

There is another fossilised tree, this time in the open, in Househill Park.

FAMOUS TREES

Mary, Queen of Scots is supposed to have nursed her husband Lord Darnley below the branches of a sycamore tree in 1567. Tests on the 'Darnley Sycamore', which stands off Nitshill Road, show that it was actually planted in about 1800.

A sweetheart rendezvous near the Pear-Tree Well on the banks of the Kelvin became known as Catherine Clark's Tree when her body was found buried there following an assignation with her swain. The tree and the well were swept away by railway development.

PLANT LIFE

In 2004 the wild plant conservation charity Plantlife asked each of the country's counties to nominate its representative flower. Glaswegians chose broom, for its bright yellow flowers had brightened the banks of the Clyde for centuries – hence 'The Broomielaw'.

When the Singer factory was destroyed during the Clydebank blitz, the ruins were quickly colonised by rosebay willow-herb. The dusky pink flowers spread rapidly over the nation's bombsites, and on Clydeside was known as Singerweed.

John Claudius Loudon (1783–1843), author of *The Encyclopaedia of Gardening* and one of the most famous garden designers of his time, was born in Cambuslang.

January 1825 was exceptionally mild. By the 7th of the month all the spring plants were in full bloom, and Glasgow gardens were abuzz with bees.

In 1995 the *Glasgow Herald* announced the city was importing tropical heat-generating domestic plants to warm the cold Glasgow tenements. Each example of *Solar Complexus Americanus* was supposed to generate 2kw of energy a day, eliminating the need for electric fires and central heating. The professor of botany who had discovered the plants was Olaf Lipro – which happened to be an anagram of April Fool.

THE ANIMAL KINGDOM

Medieval reindeer bones were found in Queen's Park during an archaeological dig in 1988.

The last recorded polecat in the Glasgow area was seen in 1868.

On 14 November 1996 a fox ran onto the pitch at Parkhead during an Old Firm game. After covering more than two-thirds of the ground it vanished into a corner exit. Play resumed after a delay of 48 seconds, Rangers beating Celtic 1–0.

On 18 August 2010 Gandalf, a female Ruppell's Griffon vulture, flew off from the World of Wings birds of prey centre in Cumbernauld and became a threat to the airspace around Glasgow and Cumbernauld airports. With a 10ft wingspan and a maximum flying height of 36,000ft, a collision with the bird could have been catastrophic, and all pilots were put on alert. After three days the errant Gandalf was safely recaptured near Falkirk.

In the 1950s the preserved corpse of a 59-ton blue whale caught off Trondheim was a popular tourist attraction outside the Kelvingrove Museum. Inevitably, the whale was named Jonah. People queued for hours to walk through the inside of the gutted and refrigerated leviathan.

Bearsden, originally known as New Kilpatrick, is thought by some to have been named after a local house where a bear was kept as a pet. Unfortunately for this piece of fanciful folk etymology, there is no evidence for any such bear.

After a long absence caused by pollution, hunting and habitat disturbance, otters have recently returned to the Clyde, Kelvin, White Cart Water and the Forth and Clyde Canal.

Glasgow contains five nationally important Sites of Special Scientific Importance (SSSIs), and seven local nature reserves. In addition there are forty-nine Sites of Importance for Nature Conservation.

In the 1960s a porpoise was found in a forgotten sack in the gents toilet of Central station. It was never claimed and its skeleton is in the Kelvingrove Museum. Please, no jokes along the lines of 'I've lost my porpoise in life.'

A Scottish wildcat was last spotted on Gleniffer Braes near Paisley in 1895. The species has long since vanished from the Lowlands.

In 1894 a Labrador dog named Wallace followed the horse-drawn fire-engine back to the Central fire station, and became adopted as the service's mascot. He attended many fires, running in front of the engines. After he died in 1902 he was stuffed and put on display alongside a pair of rubber boots made to protect his paws. Wallace became the star of a series of children's books with titles such *Wallace the Fire Dog* and *Wallace Loses his Boots*. He is currently in storage in the Glasgow Museums Resource Centre in Nitshill.

ZOOS AND MENAGERIES

Several alpacas were on display during the tenth meeting of the British Association for the Advancement of Science, held in Glasgow in 1840. In the same year a 'Zoological Garden' was briefly opened at Cranstonhill in Anderston. As well as the alpacas, visitors could see a golden eagle, a pig-tailed ape and an Indian goat.

The limited attractions of Cranstonhill were eclipsed by the wonders of the travelling menageries, which specialised in 'capital' animals such as lions, elephants and bears. A frequent visitor was George Wombwell's celebrated menagerie, which often occupied part of Glasgow Green over the summer months.

Monkeys and apes were kept for a time in the Botanic Gardens. In 1851 a baboon escaped and bit a young woman.

An entrepreneur was coining it in 1835 by exhibiting a rhinoceros in Virginia Street over Christmas.

In 1897 the showman E.H. Bostock opened the Scottish Zoo and Variety Circus, the city's first proper zoo. The venue on New City Road in Cowcaddens was one of the many entertainment projects run by the flamboyant Bostock. One of the star attractions was Sir Roger, a large male Indian elephant. He became fatally dangerous to those around him and had to be shot by a squad of soldiers. His massive bulk is a favourite with children visiting Kelvingrove Museum. Look closely and you can see that his tusks are wooden, the ivory originals having been removed when he was alive.

The Scottish Zoo closed in 1909, but Bostock continued to run travelling menageries, which were often exhibited at Kelvin Hall during the Christmas season.

From 1908 there was also a menagerie in the basement of A.E. Pickard's multi-storeyed Panopticon on Trongate, where animals were exhibited in squalid conditions. One of the star attractions was Solomon the chimpanzee, also known as 'The Man-Monkey' or 'Darwin's Missing Link'. Solomon usually wore clothes (including a top hat and tails) and stood on his hind legs when shown to visitors.

The Wilson family's miniature zoo and pet shop operated out of a disused church on Oswald Street near Central station from 1936 until the 1950s. It is best remembered for a mynah bird that said, 'Where's the sawdust man?' in a strong local accent.

In the 1950s large African and Asian animals were on display at Craigend Castle near Milngavie.

GLASGOW ZOO

Glasgow Zoo opened in Calderpark near Baillieston in 1947. The first specimen donated was a macaw named Robert.

Over 100,000 people visited the zoo in its first three weeks, most arriving by tram.

Film star endorsements included Gracie Fields naming a pair of hyenas, and four lion cubs being christened by Margaret Lockwood.

In the early years wallabies, raccoons and sealions escaped into the surrounding area. The North Calder Water flowed through the zoo to the Clyde, making for an ideal route for freedom-seeking seals.

On 5 November 1949 a tigress named Sheila got out of her cage and had to be shot. Zoo gardener Alex Innes was awarded the George Medal for protecting the big cat's keeper, John Duffy.

In 1991 the zoo received 140,000 visitors and was lauded for its research into animal behaviour.

After a tempestuous and debt-ridden final decade, the zoo closed in 2003.

FISH

Glasgow is the only Scottish conurbation with a salmon on its coat of arms.

Salmon have returned to parts of the Clyde as the environment has been cleaned up. Upstream of the weir in the city centre can also be found sea and brown trout, eels, roach, lampreys, minnow and sticklebacks, while salmon, sea trout, flounders, mullet, lampreys and silver eels swim downriver of the weir.

One Victorian newspaper letter-writer was concerned about man-eating sharks becoming active in the river, and recommended that the Clyde steamers towed fully baited shark hooks.

In 1899 a policeman found a dead shark in the street. The 8ft creature was duly loaded onto the 'drunk barrow' and wheeled to the central police station.

BIBLIOGRAPHY

Anon, *Scott & Scotland: Or, Historical and Romantic Scottish Story*, H.I. & A. Stevens, London 1845

Aird, Andrew, *Glimpses of old Glasgow*, Aird & Coghill, Glasgow, 1894

Alison, Robert, *Anecdotage of Glasgow Comprising Anecdotes and Anecdotal Incidents of the City of Glasgow and Glasgow Personages*, Morison, Glasgow, and Simpkin, Marshall, London, 1892

Automobile Association, *Secret Britain*, Automobile Association, Basingstoke, 1986

Barbe, Louis A., *In Byways of Scottish History*, Blackie & Son, London & Glasgow, 1912

Baxter, Neil (ed.), *A Tale of Two Towns: A History of Medieval Glasgow*, Neil Baxter Associates, Glasgow, 2007

Berry, Simon and Whyte, Hamish (eds), *Glasgow Observed*, John Donald, Edinburgh, 1987

Bowers, Judith, *Stan Laurel and Other Stars of the Panopticon: The Story of the Britannia Music Hall*, Birlinn, Edinburgh, 2007

Brookmyre, Christopher, *A Big Boy Did It And Ran Away*, Abacus, London, 2001

——, *The Sacred Art of Stealing*, Abacus, London, 2002

——, *Attack of the Unsinkable Rubber Ducks*, Abacus, London, 2007

Brotchie, T.C., *The History of Govan*, Old Govan Club, Glasgow, 1938

Bruce, David, *Scotland The Movie*, Polygon, Edinburgh, 1996

Burgess, Moira, *The Glasgow Novel*, Scottish Library Association, Motherwell, 1986

——, *Reading Glasgow*, Book Trust Scotland, Edinburgh, 1996

——, *Imagine a City! Glasgow in Fiction*, Argyll Publishing, Glendaruel, 1998

Callant, A.G., *Saint Mungo's Bells: Or Old Glasgow Stories Rung Out Anew*, David Bryce, Glasgow, 1888

Cant, Ronald G. and Lindsay, Ian G., *Old Glasgow,* Oliver and Boyd, Edinburgh, 1947

Carnegie, Liz; Dunlop, Harry; Jeffrey, Susan and O'Neill, Mark, *The People's Palace Book of Glasgow*, Mainstream Publishing, Edinburgh, 1998

Chambers, Robert, *Domestic Annals of Scotland from the Reformation to the Revolution* (3 vols), W. & R. Chambers, Edinburgh and London, 1859

Cleland, James, *Annals of Glasgow* (2 vols), James Hedderwick/The Glasgow Royal Infirmary, Glasgow, 1816

Cochrane, Hugh, *Glasgow – the first 800 years*, City of Glasgow District Council, Glasgow, 1975

Cooper, Quentin and Sullivan, Paul, *Maypoles, Martyrs & Mayhem*, Bloomsbury, London, 1994

Costello, Seán and Johnstone, Tom (eds), *Famous Last Words: Two Centuries of Obituaries from the Scotsman*, Mercat Press, Edinburgh, 1996

Craik, Sir Henry, *A Century of Scottish History From The Days Before The '45 To Those Within Living Memory*, Vol. I, William Blackwood & Sons, Edinburgh and London, 1901

Crawfurd, George, *The History of the Shire of Renfrew*, Alex. Weir, Paisley, 1782

Douglas, David, *Early Travellers In Scotland*, James Maclehose & Sons, Glasgow, 1891

Eunson, Eric, *The Gorbals: An Illustrated History*, Richard Stenlake Publishing, Ochiltree, 1996

Fawcett, Richard, *Scottish Cathedrals*, Batsford Ltd/Historic Scotland, London, 1997

Fisher, Joe, *The Glasgow Encyclopedia*, Mainstream Publishing, Edinburgh, 1994

Forbes, Alexander Penrose (ed.), *The Lives of S. Ninian and S. Kentigern Compiled in the Twelfth Century*, Edmonston and Douglas, Edinburgh, 1874

Foreman, Carol, *Glasgow Curiosities*, John Donald, Edinburgh, 1998

Fraser-Mackintosh, Charles, 'Incidents in the Risings of 1715 and 1745', in *Transactions of The Gaelic Society of Glasgow*, Vol. 2, 1891–4

Geikie, Sir Archibald, *Scottish Reminiscences*, James Maclehose & Sons, Glasgow, 1908

Geographers' A–Z Map Co., *A–Z Glasgow*, Geographers' A–Z Map Co., Sevenoaks, 2009

Grant, Douglas, *The Thin Blue Line: The Story of the City of Glasgow Police*, John Long, London, 1973

Gray, Muriel, *Kelvingrove Art Gallery and Museum: Glasgow's Portal to the World*, Glasgow Museums, Glasgow, 2006

Groome, Francis H. (ed.), *The Ordnance Gazetteer of Scotland: A Survey of Scottish Topography, Statistical, Biographical and Historical*, Grange Publishing Works, Edinburgh, 1882–5

Haining, Peter, *The Jail That Went To Sea: An Untold Story of the Battle of the Atlantic, 1941–42*, Conway, London, 2007

Harris, Paul, *Glasgow & The Clyde At War*, Archive Publications, Bowden, 1986

Harvey, Wallace, *Chronicles of Saint Mungo: Antiquities and Traditions of Glasgow*, John Smith & Son, Glasgow/William Blackwood & Sons, London & Edinburgh, 1843

Harvie, David, *Lines Around The City*, Lindsay Publications, Glasgow, 1997

Hayward, James, *Myths & Legends of the First World War*, Sutton, Stroud, 2002

Hill, Frederic, *Crime: Its Amount, Causes, and Remedies*, Woodfall & Kinder, London, 1853

Hone, William, *The Every-Day Book Table Book etc.* (3 vols), Thomas Tegg, London, 1827

Hothersall, Susan, *Archaeology Around Glasgow*, Glasgow Museums and Glasgow Archaeological Society, Glasgow, 2007

Holder, Geoff, *The Guide to Mysterious Glasgow*, The History Press, Stroud, 2009

House, Jack, *Square Mile of Murder*, W. & R. Chambers, Edinburgh, 1961

——, *Portrait of the Clyde*, Robert Hale & Co, London, 1969

——, *The Heart of Glasgow*, Richard Drew Publishing, Glasgow, 1972

Jeffrey, Andrew, *This Time of Crisis: Glasgow, the West of Scotland and the North Western Approaches in the Second World War*, Mainstream Publishing, Edinburgh, 1993

Johnston, James B., *Place-Names of Scotland*, James Maclehose & Sons, Glasgow, 1892

Kenna, Rudolph, *Heart of the Gorbals*, Fort Publishing, Ayr, 2004

——, & Sutherland, Ian, *In Custody: A Companion to Strathclyde Police Museum*, Strathclyde Police and Clutha Books, Glasgow, 1998

——, *They Belonged to Glasgow: The City from the Bottom Up*, Neil Wilson Publishing, Glasgow, 2001

Kielty, Martin, *SAHB Story: The Tale of the Sensational Alex Harvey Band*, Neil Wilson Publishing, Glasgow, 2004

——, *Big Noise: The Sound of Scotland*, Black & White Publishing, Edinburgh, 2006

Kilpatrick, James A., *Literary Landmarks of Glasgow*, Saint Mungo Press, Glasgow, 1897

MacDonald, Hugh, *Rambles Round Glasgow: Descriptive, Historical and Traditional*, John Smith & Son, Glasgow, 1910 (originally published 1854)

MacDougall, Carl, *Writing Scotland: How Scotland's Writers Shaped the Nation*, Polygon, Edinburgh, 2004

Macgeorge, Andrew, *Old Glasgow: The Place And The People, From The Roman Occupation To The Eighteenth Century*, Blackie And Son, Glasgow, 1880

MacKenzie, Peter, *Reminiscences of Glasgow and the West of Scotland*, John Tweed, Glasgow, 1865–8

MacLeod, Innes and Gilroy, Margaret, *Discovering The River Clyde*, John Donald Publishers Ltd, Edinburgh, 1991

McCallum, John, *The Long Way Home: The Other Great Escape*, Birlinn, Edinburgh, 2005

McKenzie, Ray, *Sculpture in Glasgow: An Illustrated Handbook*, The Foulis Archive Press, Glasgow, 1999

——, *Public Sculpture of Glasgow*, Liverpool University Press, Liverpool, 2002

McUre, John, *The History of Glasgow*, MacVean & Wylie & Co., Glasgow, 1830

Malloch, D. Macleod, *The Book of Glasgow Anecdote*, T.N. Foulis, London and Edinburgh, 1912

Mann, Ludovic Maclellan, *Earliest Glasgow, A Temple of the Moon*, The Mann Publishing Company, Glasgow and London, 1938

——, *The Druid Temple Explained*, The Mann Publishing Company, London and Glasgow, 1939

Marshall, Ian and Smith, Ronald, *Queen's Park: Historical Guide and Heritage Walk*, Glasgow City Council, Glasgow, 1997

Matheson, Alex, *Glasgow's Other River: Exploring the Kelvin*, Fort Publishing, Ayr, 2000

Maxwell, Sir Herbert, *Scottish Land-Names Their Origin And Meaning*, William Blackwood & Sons, Edinburgh, 1894

Mina, Denise, *John Constantine: Hellblazer: Empathy is the Enemy*, Vertigo, New York, 2006

——, *John Constantine: Hellblazer: The Red Right Hand*, Vertigo, New York, 2007

Mort, Frederick, *Lanarkshire*, Cambridge University Press, Cambridge, 1910

——, *Renfrewshire*, Cambridge University Press, Cambridge, 1919

Munro, John Neil, *The Sensational Alex Harvey*, Polygon, Edinburgh, 2008

Murray, Bill, *Glasgow's Giants: 100 Years of the Old Firm*, Mainstream Publishing, Edinburgh, 1988

O'Brien, Ged, *Played in Glasgow: Charting the Heritage of a City at Play*, Malavan Media/Played in Britain, London, 2010

Olcott, Charles S., *The Country of Sir Walter Scott*, Houghton Mifflin, Boston and New York, 1913

Osborne, Brian D. and Armstrong, Ronald, *Glasgow: A City At War*, Birlinn, Edinburgh, 2003

Paterson, Bill, *Tales from the Back Green*, Hodder & Stoughton, London, 2008

Phillips, Alastair, *Glasgow's Herald: Two Hundred Years of a Newspaper 1783–1983*, Richard Drew Publishing, Glasgow, 1983

Pococke, Richard, *Tours In Scotland 1747, 1750, 1760*, The Scottish History Society, Edinburgh, 1887

Ramsay, Dean, *Reminiscences of Scottish Life & Character*, T.K. Foulis, Edinburgh, 1908

Ritchie, Graham J.N. and Adamson, H.C., 'Knappers, Dunbartonshire: a reassessment' in *Proceedings of the Society of Antiquaries of Scotland* Vol. III, 1981

Rogers, Charles, *A Century of Scottish Life. Memorials and Recollections of Historical and Remarkable Persons*, Charles Griffin & Co., London, 1872

Roughead, William, *Classic Crimes: A Selection from the Works of William Roughead*, New York Review of Books Classics, New York, 2000

Scott, Sir Walter, *Rob Roy*, Signet Classics, Harmondsworth, 1995 (originally published 1817)

——, *The History Of Scotland*, Carey & Lea, Philadelphia, 1830

——, *The Talisman*, Collins, London and Glasgow, 1832

Smart, Aileen, *Villages of Glasgow: North of the Clyde*, John Donald, Edinburgh, 2002

——, *Villages of Glasgow: South of the Clyde*, John Donald, Edinburgh, 2002

Somerville, Thomas, *George Square, Glasgow: and the Lives of Those Whom its Statues Commemorate*, John N. Mackinlay, Glasgow, 1891

Spence, Lewis, 'Mythology and St Mungo' in *Scots Magazine*, 46:2, 1946

Stuart, Robert, *Views and Notices of Glasgow in Former Times*, Robert Stuart, Glasgow/Bell & Bradfute, Edinburgh, 1848

Terry, Stephen, *The Glasgow Almanac: An A–Z of the City and its People*, Neil Wilson Publishing, Glasgow, 2005

Thomas, John, *The Springburn Story: The History of the Scottish Railway Metropolis*, David & Charles, Newton Abbot, 1974

Watson, John, *Once Upon a Time in Glasgow: The City from the Earliest Times*, Neil Wilson Publishing, Glasgow, 2003